THE CHURCH CANNOT REMAIN SILENT

Unpublished Letters and Other Writings

OSCAR ROMERO

Translated by Gene Palumbo and Dinah Livingstone

ORBIS BOOKS
Maryknoll, New York 10545

Translation copyright © 2016 by Orbis Books.

Originally published in Italian as *La Chiesa Non Può Stare Zitta: Scritti Inediti 1977–1980* edited by Jesús Delgado, © 2015 by Editrice Missionaria Italiana, Via di Corticella 179/4 40128, Bologna, Italy.

This edition is translated from the original Spanish text. Letters by Oscar Romero were translated by Gene Palumbo (with invaluable assistance from Thomas Quigley). Commentary was translated by Dinah Livingstone.

The introduction is adapted from *Beato Oscar Romero* by Angelo Amato, copyright © 2015 by Libreria Editrice Vaticana, used with permission.

Romero's final Sunday homily is reprinted from Jim Wallis and Joyce Holly-day, eds., *Cloud of Witnesses* (Maryknoll, NY: Orbis Books, 2005). Romero's last homily is reprinted from Archbishop Oscar Romero, *Voice of the Voiceless* (Maryknoll, NY: Orbis Books, 1985).

Published by Orbis Books, Box 302, Maryknoll, NY 10545-0302.

Manufactured in the United States of America.

Library of Congress Cataloging-in-Publication Data

Name: Romero, Oscar A. (Oscar Arnulfo), 1917–1980. | Delgado, Jesús, editor.
Title: The church cannot remain silent : unpublished letters and writings, 1977–1980 / Oscar Romero ; edited with commentary by Jesús Delgado ; translated by Gene Palumbo and Dinah Livingstone.
Description: Maryknoll : Orbis Books, 2016.
Identifiers: LCCN 2015033373 | ISBN 9781626981751 (pbk.)
Subjects: LCSH: Romero, Oscar A. (Oscar Arnulfo), 1917–1980.—Correspondence.
Classification: LCC BX4705.R669 A25 2016 | DDC 282.092—dc23 LC record available at http://lccn.loc.gov/2015033373

*This book is affectionately dedicated to all those who,
no matter how, valued Monseñor Romero
and the way he did his pastoral job in the
archdiocese of San Salvador.*

*It is also dedicated with Christian love to all those
who didn't appreciate him, who had a grudge
against him, or simply wished him harm.*

*So that those who loved him may value him
all the more; those who didn't know him may
come to know him better; and those who hated him
during his lifetime may feel his love for them.*

CONTENTS

PREFACE

No one can fail to be aware of the extraordinary greatness that shone from the person of Monseñor Romero. His life is the story of a special calling God sent to a special person for a special time.

His character as a man of the church is well known for the service he offered both to the poor and the rich; and for the prophetic mission he carried out at a critical moment in the history of El Salvador, calling all to conversion and all to lend their voices to God to defend the defenseless, the marginalized, and the persecuted in Salvadoran society.

By his prophetic proclamation Monseñor Romero roused the conscience of a whole people suffering a living death; and he began writing with his blood the gospel of liberation from the sin that had enslaved his people, the people of God, for whom he had dedicated his life as a priest.

Monseñor Romero Was a Prophet

We should bear in mind that this Salvadoran prophet of the 1970s didn't come from the laity in the church but from the priesthood. This isn't just an interesting fact about his life but essential for understanding his character, since it is the key to understanding his message and his work.

Monseñor Romero was a priest first and foremost. At first he was deep in books and papers; then hobnobbing with high society in order to build a cathedral. Finally, God set him in the heart of the masses as their archbishop in the archdiocese of San Salvador, to be his prophet to the people of El Salvador. His homilies date from that time. They contain the core of the prophetic message that the Lord put into his mouth.

Were his homilies a loud speaker for ideas that others had suggested to him, as some people have thought, or were they the expression of his personal convictions?

Monseñor Romero's private correspondence will help us answer that question.

The Correspondence

We have a record of Monseñor Romero's copious correspondence: more than five thousand letters.

We may omit the official correspondence, which the archbishop maintained with organs of the church and state. We may also disregard the administrative and legal correspondence that arose from his position as archbishop of a diocese. We are left with the strictly personal correspondence.

Private correspondence is interesting for what it tells us about a person's feelings and ideas—sometimes their most intimate ones. This kind of correspondence is seldom used for propaganda or for self-defense against accusations.

As they are essentially written documents, Monseñor Romero's personal letters introduce us into a different psychological space from that of the homilies. They offer rich material to help us discover the faith and convictions underlying Monseñor Romero's prophetic commitment, particularly the theological approach upon which he based his hope as a man of the church.

Method

The method Monseñor Romero employed to reply personally to his correspondents was as follows.

He had a private secretary. It was usually she who opened the letters, at least those marked "Confidential," "Strictly Confidential," or the like, on the envelope. When she had opened and read the letter, the secretary wrote at the top of it in pencil a summary of its contents or a word describing its purpose, for example: "solidarity," "asks for advice," "anonymous threat," etc.

Next, Monseñor Romero received the bundle of letters, classified according to their purpose or contents. He reviewed them personally and immediately returned those that only required a formal reply to the secretary. He kept the ones needing a personal answer.

Then the archbishop handwrote on a white card the nitty gritty of the reply he wanted to give to the letter-writer. He then gave it back to the secretary for her to type up his reply onto a sheet of writing paper, between the usual heading and the foot of the page or greeting at the end. When she had finished typing his letters, the secretary gave them back to the archbishop, who read them through and signed them.

The archbishop had the secretary keep a copy of each of his reply letters, in order to file them.

This Book

This material brings us closer to Monseñor Romero and his rich personality, giving us a glimpse into this private, hidden part of his life, enabling us to see and know him better.

It is impressive to discover the trust that the faithful in the archdiocese and other dioceses of El Salvador had in Monseñor Romero. This is something that has rarely happened in the history of the church in El Salvador; it is a *kairos*, a moment of drawing nearer to God.

Usually, people presume that bishops are busy with a thousand things, and so they don't dare to write to them. Besides, not long ago ordinary people saw their archbishops hobnobbing with the powerful sectors of society; some of them were, they thought, fairly remote from the joys, hopes, and fears of the poor.

On the other hand, the people of God felt Monseñor was very close to them, concerned with their pains and fears, seeing their situation with humanity and appreciating their aspirations with Christian kindness. This archbishop used his position in the church to be a voice of the voiceless and to call to conversion those to whom God had given power, wealth, and knowledge, in order to serve the lowliest among the people.

From every direction and region of El Salvador, both Catholics and non-Catholics filled Monseñor Romero's study with letters containing their complaints and pains, their fears and hopes, their joys and their despair. The people felt Monseñor Romero's loving closeness in an even more intimate and personal way when they asked for advice, light, comfort, strength, and courage to remain steadfast in the faith, and they received his replies.

*

Order and Use of the Material

In using this material, we shall divide it into two sections: *Thoughts* and *Advice*. Needless to say, this division is merely a practical one; it is not always easy to distinguish one from another. Naturally, some ideas and concepts are repeated. That is inevitable given that the thoughts are from different letters. But when thoughts and advice are repeated, the reader will find variations and new touches.

We shall take the core of each letter, leaving out the greetings, introductions, and final salutations. We shall also respect the privacy of the people to whom he replied. So in the notes we shall cite the source as follows: Letter to—(first name and surname initial); (day the letter was answered), of—(year). (In the case of particularly private letters, we have omitted the final initials.)

A final section, drawing on Monseñor Romero's final homilies, reflects the culmination of his ministry as priest and prophet.

What Message Do Monseñor Romero's Personal Letters Contain?

Monseñor Romero's personal letters contain exactly the same message as his Sunday sermons. They proclaim a God who saves by means of his son Jesus Christ, in the church he himself founded. They also denounce the false gods who try to dethrone God and impose their destructive reign in people's homes, to corrupt their very hearts.

Monseñor Romero was the voice of God trying to stop the avalanche of false gods in El Salvador. His voice became the voice of a prophet who tries to save people from idolatrous materialism and keep their hope in the single savior God. He tried to make Salvadorans return to seeing each other as brothers and sisters; to make the capitalists realize the danger of slavery that comes from the idolatry of false gods: wealth accumulated in the hands of the few, their arrogance and abuse of power against the poorer and the defenseless in society.

This same message permeates Monseñor Romero's personal letters, with the only difference that their content is expressed in a more personal way, although keeping to the same conversational tone with his people that characterized his homilies.

May this book strengthen our faith, help us to know ourselves better and to create amongst us the loving community that Jesus so much desired.

INTRODUCTION

Blessed Oscar Romero

Cardinal Angelo Amato
Prefect for the Congregation for the Causes of Saints

The Murder of the Archbishop:
March 24, 1980

On the afternoon of March 24, 1980, the archbishop of San Salvador, Oscar Arnulfo Romero Galdámez (1917–1980), was saying Mass in the chapel of the Divine Providence Hospital where he was living. It was a Requiem Mass attended by the dead person's family and some of the hospital inpatients. The homily was a sermon on the life of every Christian, "purified," "illuminated," "transfigured" until the definitive meeting with Christ in heaven.

While preparing to begin the Offertory, the archbishop was hit in the chest and killed by a bullet shot from a car parked in front of the main chapel door. The autopsy found a small hole in his thorax. The bullet had not left the body but exploded into fragments that caused a mortal internal hemorrhage. First aid given by nurses and doctors was to no avail. It was 6:25 p.m.

Thus a witness to the gospel was mowed down by the enemies of good. He was a friend of the poor and the little people, a brave pastor in defense of freedom, justice, and peace in his country.

The funeral took place on Palm Sunday, March 30, 1980, in the cathedral square and was attended by more than 50,000 of the faithful, including priests, monks, and nuns, about twenty bishops, the Apostolic Nuncio Emmanuele Gerada, and Cardinal Ernesto Corripio Ahumada from Mexico City, representing the pope. Many journalists were also present, but the civil and diplomatic authorities did not attend for fear of attacks. In fact, the funeral was devastated by an explosion followed by gunfire. Amid the terror and general confusion more than twenty people were killed and numerous were injured. The casket was immediately removed to safety in the cathedral.

A few years later the United Nations El Salvador Truth Commission (1992–1993) managed to discover who had given the precise instructions to carry out the killing of Romero. An important witness was the driver of a four-door red Volkswagen who brought the sniper to the hospital chapel. When they arrived at the chapel, the unknown passenger—a tall, good-looking, bearded young man about twenty-five years old—told the driver to pretend to be repairing the car. Shortly afterwards a single, high velocity bullet was shot, murdering the archbishop. The driver turned around when it was fired, because he could smell gunfire. He saw the killer, sitting near the right rear window, holding a precision rifle in both hands. A professional assassin, the young man calmly ordered him to start the engine and drive slowly off. The driver concluded by saying that he had taken the killer to his superior, to whom the unknown young man said, *"misión cumplida"* ("mission accomplished").[1]

So now we ask: who was Archbishop Romero? Why was he murdered on the afternoon of March 24, 1980? What was the purpose of this diabolical act? By what reasoning can we conclude that Romero's murder was *in odium fidei*?[2] How should we judge some testimonies

---

[1] The mysterious sniper was later identified but never indicted for lack of evidence.

[2] *Editor's note*: Traditionally, a martyr is a Christian who is killed *"in odium fidei"*—in hatred of the faith. For many years those who opposed the canonization of Oscar Romero claimed that his death was not prompted by *odium fidei* but by the fact that he had mixed himself up in "politics." In 2015 Pope Francis accepted the conclusions of the Congregation for the Causes of Saints and decreed that Romero was indeed a martyr who had died *"in odium fidei."* As Archbishop Vincenzo Paglia, the postulator for the cause, observed, Romero's death "was not caused by motives that were simply political, but by hatred for a faith that, imbued with charity, would not be silent in the face

against his martyrdom? Were there difficulties that slowed down the progress of his cause?

Romero, a Priest and
Bishop Close to His People

Blessed Oscar Arnulfo Romero was born into a Catholic family in Ciudad Barrios (El Salvador) on August 15, 1917. He was the second of seven children. He grew up in a sound religious environment. He began his education in his native city. When he was twelve years old he entered the San Miguel Diocesan Seminary and at twenty he attended the Colegio Pio Latino Americano in Rome. From 1937 to 1943 he pursued philosophical and theological studies at the Gregorian University. He was ordained a priest in Rome on April 4, 1942. Summoned home by his bishop during World War II in August 1943, he finally arrived after several adventures, including three months served in a Cuban prison, accused of spying.

From 1947 to 1967 he worked as a priest in the city of San Miguel, first as a country priest and then in the city center. He was also the bishop's secretary, chancellor, vicar general, director of the diocesan seminary, rector of the minor seminary, president of the committee for building

---

of the injustices that relentlessly and cruelly slaughtered the poor and their defenders." Romero was officially beatified—the last stage prior to canonization—in a ceremony in San Salvador on May 23, 2015.

the cathedral, and a teacher of religion and morals. He was spiritual director to numerous religious men and women. He belonged to many groups and church movements in the diocese: Catholic Action, Legion of Mary, Guard of the Blessed Sacrament, Franciscan Third Order, Knights of the Holy Sepulcher, *Cursillos de Cristiandad, Movimiento Familiar Cristiano,* and Alcoholics Anonymous.

In 1967 he was moved to the capital, San Salvador, with the job of Secretary to the Salvadoran Bishops' Conference. He was ordained bishop on November 21, 1970, as auxiliary of San Salvador. In 1974 he became bishop of Santiago de María and in 1977 archbishop of San Salvador as successor to Monseñor Luis Chávez González.

A man of prayer and deep spirituality, Romero fulfilled these many tasks with simplicity and in a spirit of service and sacrifice. His passion was helping those living in poverty, and he was close to his oppressed and downtrodden people. He was welcoming and kind to beggars and to prisoners whom he regularly visited.

Heroic Pastor

As archbishop Monseñor Romero exercised his pastoral ministry at a time when the society of El Salvador was beset by deep political rivalries and polarized into many right- and left-wing factions. He invited all to conversion, kindness, and peace. He tried to instill a Christian social conscience, especially in those who had received

great wealth from God and therefore had certain political, social, and economic responsibilities in the country.

He called upon the rich and powerful to undergo a
change of heart, not to lull their consciences merely by
outwardly pious practices but by truly respecting social
justice and the rights of the poorest. He asked the poor to
avoid any form of violent revolution, encouraging them
to organize politically in order to seek possible solutions
for the country's grave social problems. He asked both
rich and poor to mend their ways, for forgiveness, kindness, peace, and justice. Their ideal should be to follow
Christ the Savior from whom their country's name El
Salvador derived.

His invitation was not properly understood; and his
religious activity was often adjudged to be political and
socialist rather than pastoral in its intent.

On the one hand the country's traditionally powerful
sectors felt they were being attacked because until then no
one had dared to criticize their arrogance and abuses. On
the other hand the poor, kept down by fear and ongoing
repression, heard in Romero a voice speaking for them.

Romero knew well the church's social doctrine and
maintained close links with the pope and the Holy See,
as evidenced by the texts of his speeches and homilies. He
particularly venerated Pope Paul VI, and he had time in
just a few meetings to get to know John Paul II. On January 30, 1980, he said in his Sunday homily: "Brothers and
sisters, a pastor's greatest glory is to live in communion

with the pope. For me, the secret of the truth and efficacy of my preaching is that it is in communion with the pope."

Threatened with death by the country's powerful oligarchy, Romero was murdered on March 24, 1980. He fell dead before the altar and the Blessed Sacrament. For Salvadorans the spot became a sign of God's acceptance of his self-sacrifice for the church for the salvation of souls and the building of the reign of Christ, a reign of justice, truth, love, and peace.

A Society Riven by Discord

Along with El Salvador's difficult socio-political situation, its history must be examined to better understand the *odium fidei* nurtured in the hearts and minds of Romero's persecutors. In 1825, after three centuries of Spanish rule, the state of El Salvador became independent.

However, a small number of families took possession of the cultivable land, grabbing it from the indigenous people. As a result, while the big landowners profited from the coffee plantations and the sale of this precious product, the peasants and the rest of the population remained in poverty.

The situation became radicalized in the twentieth century with the polarization of social forces, roughly divided into six groups: the extreme right-wing big landowners; the industrialists, who defended the status quo; the center comprising intellectuals and technical workers who were in favor of reform; the popular left-wing movements, who promoted change; the extreme left-wing guerrillas, whose aim was the violent imposition of a communist state; and the military, who were closely linked to the rich and powerful and who oppressed the country with abuse and illegality.

Any attempt at social reform, such as that undertaken in 1972 by President Arturo Armando Molina, gave rise to fierce repression on the part of the military, which defended the status quo in favor of the rich. Meanwhile, the extreme left took advantage of the situation to unleash violence. This situation beset by opposing interests and ideologies caused a string of violent attacks on people and property, sowing destruction and death. Very often those who paid the price were priests and Catholic laity involved in social action.

The Murder of Father Rutilio Grande and Romero's "Conversion"

A key event leading up the murder of Archbishop Romero was the assassination of the Salvadoran Jesuit Rutilio Grande on March 12, 1977. He was hated by the big landowners and the military for his work promoting peasants' rights. He was killed along with two peasants on the road to Aguilares, where he lived.

Father Rutilio was a humble and kind man. He had given up academic teaching in order to live simply among the peasants. He was convinced that the only solution to the evils in his country was to spread the gospel to the poor and downtrodden. He did not take part in political projects and plans but happily spoke to the workers, exhorting them to practice Christian love.

Father Rutilio's murder profoundly shook and disturbed Archbishop Romero. He went immediately to Aguilares to celebrate Mass for the dead. He spent the night keeping vigil for the three poor victims.

That was the moment of Romero's so-called "conversion." He resolved to denounce abuses and defend the poor and priests more forcefully. Yet in an interview in March 1979 the archbishop rejected the word conversion: "I would not speak of conversion, as many call it . . . because I have always been devoted to the people and the poor." For Romero Father Rutilio Grande's death did not involve a substantial change in his ideas but an intensification of his faithfulness to the poor and a defense of the church's rights. Rather than *conversion,* he preferred to call it a special "pastoral strengthening" (*fortaleza pastoral),* which went against his conservative temperament and inclinations: "I decided it was my duty to take a firm stand to defend my church, and from within the church, stand side by side with my people who were so oppressed and abused."[3]

His decision, announced in a meeting with his priests, was a courageous choice: "I understood," he said, "that

---

[3] *Positio super martyrio* (2014), 178.

I had to take a stand, and in fact, we made a decision: to celebrate a single Mass and not allow any other Masses to be celebrated on the following Sunday. That decision cost me dearly, but it was something that had a strong impact on the diocese and helped me to feel the strength that I felt thanks to God, in communion with the priests and the community who were with me."[4] This resolute position was not a kind of retaliation against the government, but a demonstration of a preference for his priests and people, whom he was bound to protect and defend with all his strength from wicked wolves.

So he increased calls for understanding. His voice was the one most listened to in the country, to the great annoyance of the military and both right- and left-wing extremists. This resulted in pressures put on him and practical attempts to deter him. He was told to leave El Salvador. He was offered money to go abroad. Priests and catechists were persecuted and killed and sacred buildings and churches were attacked in attempts to isolate him. All to no avail, so they decided to eliminate him.

The Persecutors' Odium Fidei

In order to justify the murder, political propaganda was used to influence public opinion into believing that Romero had "converted to communism," and as such, was an enemy of public order who must be eliminated at all

---

[4] *Ibid.,* 177.

costs. But that accusation was refuted by the facts and by the archbishop's own words and life, which condemned any form of armed struggle and preached only peace and kindness. The people understood this at once.

In reality, Romero was murdered because he represented the highest religious authority with the strongest voice in defending the rights of the poor and those at the bottom of society and denouncing the abuses of the rich and powerful. It was the gospel of justice and harmony; the archbishop's *Magna Carta* for pastoral preaching and action. So he was relentlessly attacked by his persecutors precisely because his pastoral work constituted a continual reproach to their injustice and violence. They hated him because he tried to preach and practice the gospel.

As was the case for the persecutors who martyred the early Christian, so it was for Romero's murderers. They may not have had the explicit intention to deny God, but in fact their action was in open defiance of the divine commandment not to kill and Jesus's gospel of love, which also meant kindness, justice, and charity.

The instigators and perpetrators of the archbishop's murder were truly atheists and idolaters because they denied God and his law of love. For the Christian God they substituted the idols of wealth and violence, which they worshipped and upon whose altar they shamefacedly shed the blood of innocent victims (priests and poor peasants).

Hence Romero's murder was caused by this profound *odium fidei, odium evangelii, odium Ecclesiae.*

The Prophecy of Martyrdom

What about the so-called formal martyrdom of Romero? Formal martyrdom refers to Romero's state of mind with regard to facing possible martyrdom as the supreme gift of his life for the cause of peace and kindness for his people. Was Archbishop Romero prepared for martyrdom?

As a priest and bishop he had always remained faithful to the magisterium of the church, conducting his mission in accordance with the directives of the Second Vatican Council and the Latin American pastoral directives of Medellín (1968) and Puebla (1979) in defense of the poor and excluded. He felt a particular responsibility for so many people who had been exploited for centuries and kept down in a state of real social injustice. Through his pastoral work he was fully aware that he was facing persecution, hostilities, calumnies, and even death.

The danger signs were already present with the murder of Father Rutilio Grande in 1977. That episode drove Romero to demand explanations from the government and the powerful oligarchy. He got no response. The situation grew worse with the killing of Father Alfonso Navarro on May 11 of the same year along with the massacre of many civilians on May 17. Murder, violence, and all kinds of abuses continued to occur.

Romero opposed that violence, using only the weapons of faith and the gospel, inviting all to conversion and reconciliation. Some years later, in his testimony, the apostolic nuncio Archbishop Emmanuele Gerada spoke approvingly of the archbishop's work, stating that he sought every possible means to promote kindness in the Church and society. Our martyr's preaching educated people about the faith. Romero was not involved in politics and was not subversive.

In his notes on the Spiritual Exercises undertaken in February 1980, a few weeks before his murder, the archbishop said he was aware of his possible and perhaps imminent death and reaffirmed his total dedication to his flock, following the example of the Good Shepherd.[5]

On March 9, just fifteen days before his martyrdom, a bomb was found behind the pulpit at the Sacred Heart of Jesus Basilica where he had officiated a mass the previous day in memory of Mario Zamora Rivas, an attorney assassinated by the death squads. Had the attack not failed because of a technical fault in the timer of the dynamite, an unprecedented massacre would have occurred.

Despite the obvious danger, the archbishop would not keep silent. On Sunday, March 23, the eve of his death, he gave his usual homily. The homily lasted about two hours. As usual, he preached how the gospel applied to the situation, illuminated by the Church's social teaching, including a list of numerous misdeeds perpetrated by the powerful and an invitation to turn hearts of stone into hearts of flesh. At the end of the homily he issued his

---

[5] *Cuaderno no. 3 de Ejercicios* (February 25, 1980), 307.

famous invitation to the military not to obey orders that were against God's law. That was the beginning of the end.

However, Romero is not a martyr for revolution, as some tried to dub him straight after his death. Neither was he a man who wanted to put his country's safety in danger. He was simply a martyr for Christ. His words denouncing social injustice are the words of a prophet, who in God's name defends the poor and the little people against the arrogance and abuses of the powerful without heart. He is the prophet of reconciliation and social peace. He is a martyr for that revolution of love which is Christianity, which has charity in its DNA as the supreme and absolute virtue.

Some Questions

The death of Archbishop Romero was truly a credible witness to the faith, and there can be no doubt about the meaning and value of his martyrdom. In the year 2000, in an ecumenical commemoration of witnesses to the faith in the twentieth century, Pope John Paul II offered this prayer: "Father of the poor, remember those who bore witness to the truth and charity of the gospel even to offering their own lives: passionate pastors like the unforgettable Archbishop Oscar Romero, killed at the altar."[6]

And speaking of Romero in an interview given on board a flight from Rome to São Paulo in Brazil, on May

---

[6] *Positio*, 545.

9, 2007, Pope Benedict XVI said: "Monseñor Romero was certainly a great witness to the faith, a man of high Christian virtue who was devoted to the cause of peace and against the dictatorship and who was killed during the celebration of Mass."

How can we present him rightly, freeing him from attempts on the part of a political party to adopt him as their banner, their figurehead? That's the problem. This is being examined by the Congregation for the Cause of Saints.[7] A final sentence spoken by the pope was also recorded by the sixty journalists present but not reported in all the organs of the press. Literally it said: "We have no doubt that this person deserves beatification."[8]

Pope Francis gave an interview to journalists along the same lines, on board a flight from Rome to the Philippines. He spoke of Romero's imminent beatification in San Salvador (January 19, 2015).

There are certain questions that must be resolved. For example, there is the question of his relationship with those clerics who remained on good terms with the government and did not welcome the archbishop's "undiplomatic" statements against the abuses and injustices of the politicians and military. Although they respected him for his simple and virtuous life as a priest, they begged him to moderate his tone. As they did not succeed, they

---

[7] *L'Osservatore Romano* (May 11, 2007), 6.

[8] *Positio*, VI.

invited the Roman authorities to arrange apostolic visits to El Salvador or to remove Romero from the archdiocese.

Rome did send an apostolic visit but did not remove Romero from his diocese. So the archbishop continued to act, conscious that his pastoral mission was to defend the poor, the persecuted, and his priests from the oppression of the powerful.

He had further confirmation of Rome's protection when he went there to confer with Pope Paul VI. It was a meeting that made a deep impression on him. Indeed, Pope Paul VI welcomed him with fatherly affection, giving him words of comfort and encouragement. He blessed the photograph of Father Rutilio Grande that Romero showed him. He said farewell to Romero speaking in Italian in words that the archbishop would repeat several times in his homilies: "Courage, it is you who is in charge."[9]

When he arrived back at his diocese a reassured Romero publicly stated: "If I were not in communion with the pope, I would not be worthy of this honorable position of being pastor of this archdiocese. But the pope is the one to tell me so and not anyone else. And that pope has just confirmed his communion with me and mine with him. We are in communion."[10]

There are a few witnesses who considered Romero to have been a just man who invited all to kindness and

---

[9] *Ibid.,* 353.
[10] *Ibid.*

defended the poor and the persecuted but nevertheless his activity was substantially of a political nature. According to them, there was no political oppression in El Salvador and no persecution of the church.

However, these statements are belied by the evidence. The reality was quite different: "El Salvador was then in a state of civil war, with the government's activities becoming ever more oppressive, so much so that between 1977 and 1980 they caused more than 80,000 deaths. They also gave rise to a continual state of guerrilla warfare and brutal violence. Those who were targeted and persecuted were mainly the faithful and clergy, many of whom received all kinds of threats and physical and moral persecution. Fifteen percent of priests were threatened and expelled or tortured and assassinated."[11]

There are also those who reproach Romero for a lack of humility. But the evidence shows that humility also played a part in his virtuous life. Moreover, martyrdom is a real baptism of blood that wipes out the stains of the past. Speaking to the persecutors of his own time Tertullian said: "Through martyrdom all sins are forgiven. That is the reason why we thank you for condemning us. There is a contrast between the divine and the human: when we are condemned by you we are absolved by God."[12]

---

[11] *Ibid.*, IX.

[12] Tertullian, *Apologetico,* 50, 16.

The Universal Fame of his Martyrdom

The fame of Romero's martyrdom can be seen from the numerous testimonies praising his strength of spirit and courage in denouncing abuses and defending the poor and the persecuted. His murder made a deep impression not only on Catholics but also on Christians of other denominations who saw Romero as an example and inspiration.

There are also incidents of true conversions. There was the striking case of the rich Salvadoran businessman who was impressed by Romero's example and regained a committed Christian faith so that he distributed his wealth fairly and treated private property as an asset to be used for social purposes. Because of his "evangelically revolutionary" action in defense of the poor and oppressed he was assassinated.[13]

For the people Romero is a martyr and prophet, because he gave his life for the word of God and because he preached the law of charity. Since the day of his funeral, the faithful have been going to his tomb to pray to him and seek his protection. His sacrifice had an extraordinary impact on hearts and minds, especially upon Latin American bishops and priests who felt strengthened by his example and impelled to imitate him.

Today Romero is known throughout the world as a martyr for the gospel and for justice between nations.

---

[13] *Positio*, 522.

Above the Great West Door of the Anglican Westminster Abbey some statues have been erected of twentieth century Christian martyrs. Together with Martin Luther King and Dietrich Bonhoeffer, there is a statue of Romero. His statue also stands in the National Cathedral in Washington DC. On March 23, 2011, President Barack Obama paid homage at Archbishop Romero's tomb. Musicals, documentaries, and films have also been dedicated to Romero.

The particular reasons for his fame as a martyr are his love for the poor, his defense of the defenseless, his witness to Christian faith in the public life of his country, his quest for peace, and above all the fact that as a pastor he did not forsake his flock at a time of persecution when he himself was also threatened.

Romero did not die with his miter in his hand, but he was killed while saying Mass. He was a man of the church, a pastor who was obedient to the pope and his magisterium, a man of prayer, devoted to the Sacred Hearts of Jesus and Mary, an exemplary priest who "felt with the church" and who aspired to holiness.

So it is appropriate here to quote the memorial words at his funeral: "They have killed the best man, the gentlest, fairest, finest, noblest, holiest man."

He was beatified by Pope Francis on May 23, 2015.

—Translated by Dinah Livingstone

Part I

THOUGHTS

∾

The social situation in El Salvador, at such variance with the gospel teachings that Mons. Romero describes in his letters, was nothing new to him. Born in 1917, he had lived through the tumultuous era of the 1930s, when peasants rose up against the oligarchy, only to be decimated by the thousands. But much of this was occurring outside his attention, while he was hidden away in seminary. A few years later he was sent off to Rome.

When he returned from Europe in 1943 he could see what was happening, but didn't bother analyzing it; his focus, as a young priest, was on achieving personal holiness. In those years he believed that prayer was the best way for a priest to contribute to the cause of justice. He wasn't ignorant about the causes of social evil in El Salvador. He knew that it was rooted in the culture inherited

*from the time of the Spanish conquest—a culture that led
to ignominious misery for some and scandalous riches for
others. But how simply to condemn the wealthy when
they were so generous in contributing to the works of
the Church? And how to raise their social consciousness
without hurting their feelings or leading them to suspect
ideological motives? At that time, the only thing that
occurred to him was to foment the practice of charity
on the part of the rich. The only thing a priest could do
was pray.*

*He also preached. According to those who heard him
at the time, his sermons were doctrinally solid and well
presented. Nevertheless, few felt challenged by them. They
were moved to go to confession, to be more charitable
toward the poor, but never challenged by the love of God
to change social relations or the structures of society.*

*Why was he not more attentive to the signs of the
times? Perhaps he was more focused then on pursuing the
perfection of his soul and humanizing his temperament,
which he himself, in his spiritual diaries, termed "surly
and dry." But the day came when God thrust Monseñor
Romero up to his neck in the crude reality of the suffering
of a people, a suffering caused by the inhuman arrogance
of the Salvadoran power elites.*

*When Monseñor Romero took charge as pastor of
the archdiocese of San Salvador the Church Fathers and
church doctrine were no longer his only sources of inspiration for preaching; now he was inspired above all by the*

actual life of the Salvadoran people. The "composition of place" with which he began his daily Ignatian meditations began to be colored by his recognition of the shocking excesses of the rich and the sufferings of the poor. In the "petitions" of these meditations he gravitated toward asking to become an instrument of change in the life of all, to move the rich to conversion and the poor to a greater sense of solidarity with their poor brothers and sisters.

Monseñor Romero knew that he had to pronounce a "mea culpa" for the silence of church leaders who had adopted for so long an idolatrous attitude of having eyes but not seeing, having a mouth but not speaking. In pronouncing this "mea culpa," Monseñor Romero acknowledged his own sins, but he also chose the path of conversion in becoming the voice of those who have no voice.

The Church in Which We Live

El Salvador is a small country, hard-working and long-suffering. We experience here great contrasts in the life of our society, in economic, political, and cultural marginalization. In a word, INJUSTICE. The church cannot remain silent in the face of such misery, for to do so would be to betray the gospel, it would be to become complicit with those who here trample human rights. This is why the church is persecuted, its fidelity to the gospel. *(Letter to S. Wagner, February 9, 1978)*

For many years we in the church have been responsible for people seeing the church as allied with the wealthy and politically powerful, thus contributing to the injustices of the society in which we live. God speaks to us through events and persons. God spoke to us through Father Rutilio, through Father Navarro, through the farm workers, and so on. And God speaks to us through the peace and the hope that we experience even in the midst of such tribulation. *(Letter to Alfredo T., October 28, 1977)*

The present situation is truly one of great concern, with brothers and sisters engaged in bloody battles with each other. In our situation, this is due to the egoism of the powerful and wealthy. They are building a kingdom of injustice, for their actions are aimed only to preserve their own position. *(Letter to Paula J., June 31, 1977)*

Here where hunger leaves its mark in so many lives so early, children naked and malnourished, farm workers in situations of urgent need. . . . Here where injustice has to be called by its proper name, where misery has very concrete faces, and it is in this time and in this moment of our history that the Lord calls us as church to build the KINGDOM OF GOD. *(Letter to Bamdoux H., November 10, 1979)*

Here and now the local church journeys on its sorrowful Calvary, as the attacks continue on the Christians committed to raise up the gospel message to their brothers and sisters, especially in the rural areas of certain parishes, with some killed, others wounded. Therefore, I won't cease asking you to keep us in your prayers, which we so need to remain faithful. *(Letter to Diego De P., September 5, 1979)*

People are aware of our situation, some more, some less, and very few families maintain friendship, and those which could help you have lost my confidence. In light of that, I ask you to excuse me but for now I can do nothing for your situation; perhaps later. *(Letter to Aura M. Z., July 14, 1977)*

The social situation in El Salvador is tremendously unjust. We're living in social sin. The church is trying to make its voice heard everywhere that we might, as Christians, take responsibility for overcoming the sin and build a brotherhood and sisterhood based on justice. *(Letter to Johan and Clara v. B., November 10, 1977)*

The Ministry That Has Been Entrusted to Me

The ministry that Providence has decided that I exercise has been in times of greatest difficulty for this country and for the local church. They have assassinated two of our priests and taken others (although we were able to get them released). Many foreign priests have been expelled and some Salvadorans, under threat, had to leave the country. Among the general population there have been kidnappings, murders, and many disappearances. Given all this, it has fallen to me to make present the word of God.

In the midst of this tragedy, the presence of God has been marvelous. I have received support from my priests, the laypeople who do pastoral work, religious men and women, and, overall, the entire People of God. We have always sought to listen to the Holy Spirit who has clearly been manifested here.

The persecutions of the early church, those of the missions, etc., up to a certain point seem to be part of a history long past, but here we are forced to live that history with all its harshness.

I can certainly say that my conscience does not accuse me of having said or done things capriciously or under pressure or out of cowardice. On the contrary, we see the evidence in our life: an immense quantity of letters

from the humblest farm worker to church dignitaries.
On Wednesdays I have a radio program which, according to surveys, the people are listening to; the same with
the Sunday homilies, which are also broadcast. *(Letter
to Mario P., November 1, 1977)*

What graces the Lord sends us! We are able to build the
Kingdom of God together. You can't imagine how good the
Lord has been to us. Along with the stormy days come the
joyful days when we see how the Lord has aroused interest
in the apostolic work among both lay and religious men
and women. *(Letter to Joyce B., July 8, 1977)*

Cross: Time of Hope

The situation in our country is the same as it was last
year. Recently there have been more arrests, murders,
and disappearances. The Christian communities and their
leaders have been threatened. There have been military
operations and violent repression against the farm workers
in San Pedro Perulapán, San Martín, Cojutepeque, and
neighboring villages in the province of Cuscatlán.

People have been fleeing, fearing that they'll be victims
of human rights violations. The country's media—radio,
press, TV—have twisted the facts to make it appear that
activist farm workers are behind the violence, but in reality
it is the people of ORDEN [a rightist paramilitary group—
Ed.] who have caused this disorder with the support of
the authorities.

The church cannot be silent at a moment like this. We have denounced what is happening on our radio and our newspaper, which has triggered new calumnies against me and the priests of the archdiocese. We are making a plea for the cooperation of all Christians in support of those victimized.

We need your prayers to help us stay faithful to the gospel that the Lord wants us to preach. *(Letter to Arturo B., April 4, 1978)*

It's true that the situation of our church, which you know so well, is very difficult because of the conditions in which it has to carry out its mission; but at the same time, I feel very happy to belong to this archdiocese so filled with Christians trying to live their faith in solidarity with the poorest. Here the paschal mystery is a daily reality. *(Letter to Luis V. de V., April 26, 1979)*

As you say, a new mission, a new cross, and one I embrace with great trust in the Lord and with the sole desire of doing his will. And with the sure hope of the prayers of all the church, of all Christians, and our fellow bishops, the hope for a Salvadoran church made pure and more luminous through these very trials. *(Letter to Giovanni G., May 12, 1977)*

It is with great affection that I thank you for your beautiful words of solidarity in these difficult but in a certain sense glorious times, in which our church is living. For Christians of evangelical witness like yourself and so many others, faithful to the word and life of Jesus, transform sorrow into life, as did Christ. I am sure that your example and that of your family of being faithful to Christ even in the midst of persecution has to be a great light of faith there in your community. *(Letter to Felicita G. R., August 8, 1979)*

In these hours of both pain and hope for our church, to receive such evangelical words fills me with joy in the Lord. We Christians understand each other, that the cross is no defeat, for it is joined to the resurrection and is the step which precedes it. *(Letter to Carlos S., October 13, 1978)*

I am happy to congratulate you for the well-done Holy Week celebration, and I hope it has been for many a time of interior silence, of reflection and conversion. Especially that all Christians have had the profound joy of sensing the victory of the Risen Christ who overcame death itself, and all sin and evil.

The Paschal Triduum tells us of a God who lives to give us life, to tell us that in Christ we have the reason for our existence, for in him shines the hope of our own resurrection in heaven. We walk the pilgrim path of life, discovering him and loving him in our brothers and sisters. *(Letter to David F., April 26, 1979)*

Thanks then for sharing our pain, lightened up solely by the sure hope of resurrection of those who bear the palm of martyrdom. Let us encourage and console one another in our prayers each day. *(Letter to Guadalupe de J. T., August 25, 1979)*

Seedbed for Christians

Thanks be to God that my archdiocese is carrying on, united and prayerful, in spite of the repression we have been experiencing over the last two years. The blood of martyrs is the seed of Christians and the witness of priests who have died with their people because of their evangelical commitment has resulted in many priestly vocations. Both the major and minor seminaries are filled with enthusiastic young people. *(Letter to Leonel C., April 21, 1979)*

To be sure, the deaths of many brother priests and catechists due to the repression of our people and of the church which is trying to carry out its prophetic mission have been very hard for all of us. But our faith in the risen Lord helps us see the nobility of these martyrs and gives new life to our local church. *(Letter to Fr. Generoso G. C., April 19, 1979)*

In our country there is so much to lament, given that every day the spiral of violence, which is but the reflection of sin and injustice, increases. And when, in the midst of this darkness and corruption, the church seeks to be a leaven, salt and light, its priests and pastoral workers are attacked. *(Letter to Fr. Carlos G., November 18, 1979)*

The persecution we are suffering is very similar to that of the first Christian communities. Give thanks to God since we are being persecuted because we have evangelized: "Blessed are those who suffer persecution for justice's sake." I recommend reading and meditating on Matthew, chapter 10. The road the Lord offers us is hard and narrow, but happy are those who manage to pursue it to the end. Our martyrs give us the example. *(Letter to the Christian community of Zapotitán, July 4, 1979)*

In a Martyr Church

It is good to know that, from among our priests, we now have some representatives before the throne of God. *(Letter to Fr. Miguel A. R., July 17, 1979)*

We try to be faithful to our prophetic mission, which also brings us problems and calumnies. Last week another of our diocesan priests, Rafael Palacios, was murdered. *(Letter to a base community, June 26, 1979)*

Then we had the deep sorrow at the assassination of Father Alirio Macías of San Esteban Catarina. Among the people the different kinds of repression continue: torture, prison, assassinations, disappearances. There has been a great deal of blood and sacrifice which we trust will soon bear fruit in the peace, justice, and freedom that we haven't had in our country. *(Letter to Fr. Mario B., September 6, 1979)*

As for what you ask me about Fr. Rutilio Grande, you can be sure about the authentic pastoral truth of his work. All of us who knew him well saw his great human and Christian qualities. He was an exemplary priest, given to the service of his brothers and sisters in the work of evangelization.

Today some are trying to tarnish the image and memory of people like Father Rutilio, making some people believe that they had lost the gospel way. Those who are doing this are very clever, so take care. Ask the Holy Spirit to help you understand the boldness that the gospel calls for. *(Letter to Berta P. G., July 13, 1979)*

With our hope in God, we trust that Father Grande is now helping us from heaven. We should feel optimistic because the church that is persecuted is holy. *(Letter to Gonzalo P. M., March 26, 1977)*

Conversion

To be sure, for many years we in the church have been responsible for many people seeing the church as an ally of those who have political and economic power, and thus contributing to this society of injustice in which we live. But thanks to God, who is always calling us to conversion, the Salvadoran church is trying to convert to the gospels. That is our struggle right now.

Personally, I want to be a faithful and docile instrument of the work of the Holy Spirit in these times. I lend my voice to the Lord, so that I can be the voice of those who have no voice. The moment has come when we Christians must respond to the call of the Lord. There are many who still haven't awakened. Let us be patient with them. Let us pray and, insofar as we can, help them to awaken. *(Letter to Alfredo T. D., October 28, 1977)*

In this new political situation for our country, the church perseveres in its call for conversion, to bring an end to actions based on hatred and vengeance and to seek the path of justice and love as the only way to achieve authentic well-being. *(Letter to Erwin R., October 30, 1979)*

I invite you not to lose heart in your work of announcing the liberating message of Jesus for everyone. We mustn't let ourselves be discouraged by the misunderstandings of those who are not on the path of conversion. Let us strengthen ourselves for our pastoral work by praying for each other. *(Letter to Jesús L., August 25, 1979)*

Prophet and Servant

We have never discriminated against anyone. Our call to union and conversion is constant. The church has a prophetic mission: to ANNOUNCE how we should live as children of God; to DENOUNCE every type of sin (personal and social) and to call to CONVERSION. The church doesn't reject anyone, but it also doesn't oblige anyone. Conversion is an indispensable requisite to be in communion with God and with everyone. *(Letter to Maria T. P., July 4, 1979)*

Our voice as pastor of the archdiocese seeks only to be an instrument in the hands of Christ so that he can speak to his people today. We want to be faithful to the gospel, and we're aware of the consequences which that can bring. But the Lord gave us a good example, and he constantly urges us to go forward. *(Letter to Roberto M. C., November 14, 1977)*

The ministry that has been given me is, like the one given to Moses, to lead our people to the "promised land." *(Letter to Ernestina R., November 26, 1979)*

Thanks to the Lord who makes use of this humble servant to bring consolation to his most abandoned brothers and sisters. This is my mission as pastor: to give direction, to serve, to be "the voice of those who cannot speak," to denounce sin, and to announce the kingdom of God and the liberating salvation that Jesus brought us. *(Letter to José C. G., October 25, 1977)*

I have given myself only to Christ so that he can speak to the people of these times, asking them to convert and encouraging them to live according to his gospel. My voice I give to the Lord so that his people might speak. *(Letter to José Antonio M., October 31, 1977)*

With Love

I understand how you feel as a mother, but I ask you to understand my prophetic duty, which, on the basis of my fidelity to the gospel and my defense of those who have been trampled upon, obliges me to sacrifice even my personal feelings if they might weaken my Christian testimony as the person responsible for this archdiocese.

I have denounced attitudes that need to be denounced. I have done that not out of resentment, or as an irresponsible critic, but because of the very love I have for everyone, a love that demands clarity and justice. . . . If the errors committed have been public, then the call to correct them must be public, too. The call is addressed to a person who has civil authority, so that he will exercise that authority on behalf of the majority and in the service of justice. *(Letter to Ana T. de F., October 10, 1978)*

As you have seen in my homilies, the church condemns all violence, wherever it may come from. That's why we are constantly calling on both extremes to find peaceful solutions for our problems. *(Letter to Berta B. G., December 18, 1979)*

The church can't be silent when thousands of our brothers and sisters are suffering the consequences of injustice in Latin America. It can't be silent before the pain and abuses that are constantly visited on the farm workers and the people in general. The church has the firm hope that a day will come when there will be peace, justice, and love among us. That's why we're working constantly, trying to build the kingdom of God on earth. *(Letter to Antonio Z., June 14, 1978)*

When we denounce these acts against the dignity of man proclaimed by the gospel and pointed out by the magisterium, we are constantly accused and vilified, but we think with St. Paul, "I can do all things through him who strengthens me." *(Letter to Cardinal Leo Joseph Suenens, December 21, 1978)*

With Firmness

Our church is in a difficult situation because it has to live out its prophetic mission in a sinful society of social injustice, which causes problems when it denounces sin and proclaims how to live as Christians. Those not open to be converted see the church's mission as "subversive." *(Letter to Patrick F., April 19, 1979)*

They don't want even a single voice clashing with the voice of the powerful. They don't want to hear anyone defending those who have no voice, much less defending those who are helpless and persecuted. *(Letter to Mons. Leonidas Proaño, July 27, 1977)*

With the Universal Church and the Local Church

I am totally convinced that the Salvadoran people are fully aware that my only commitment is to the church. My whole life is grounded in the church's call to proclaim and denounce. Those who speculate that I have other motives are simply trying to cause confusion. *(Letter to Eduardo G., May 12, 1979)*

I am both honored and grateful for your invitation to be the main speaker at the annual meeting of the Catholic Institute for International Relations in London next June. Despite my desire to accept your kind invitation, I fear I must say no. Knowing the situation of my archdiocese and its tensions with the government, I believe that any talk I would give abroad in support of truth and justice would seem a provocation. For now, I believe that my own pulpit is the appropriate place from which to defend my people. *(Letter to Julian Filochowski, April 3, 1979)*

While I am, thank God, in good health, I am concerned. You well know the real situation here and the difficulties that, as pastor, I face from those who oppose the pastoral work of the archdiocese. But as the Lord said, "Fear not, for I am with you." And I am not discouraged, for as St. Paul said, "When I feel weak, that is when I am strongest, because the Lord shows his power in my weakness." *(Letter to Gloria C., November 11, 1979)*

It is consoling to know that the church is greater and holier when it is persecuted and that any sacrifice is worthwhile when we are the living voice of the Church of Christ. *(Letter to Fr. Pedro D., March 24, 1977)*

Pray much for our archdiocese and for me so that the Lord will give us the grace to be faithful to the mission He has given us. It's a very difficult mission, especially when the church tries to make itself heard in a society where social sin is the norm. *(Letter to Carmen E., December 8, 1977)*

With Patience

God is with us, and so our faith ought to encourage us not to take seriously these threats which unscrupulous people try to alarm us with, creating an atmosphere of anxiety. *(Letter to María Luisa A., December 14, 1979)*

Certainly, as Christians we have to exercise patience in the face of the calumnies of much of the media here which distort the truth, our witness to the truth of Christ that denounces, in word and deed, violence and exploitation. Our best response should be perseverance in this authentic evangelical course. *(Letter to Natividad A. L., July 20, 1979)*

The enemies of the message of truth, unable to take a step toward conversion, have become bearers of calumny and slander. For them we will pray constantly that in the not too distant future they may become meek before him who said "The truth will set you free." *(Letter to Guillermo N., July 20, 1979)*

Those worshippers of the worldly powers are the ones who deform the truth in their favor, no matter how clearly we speak to them. They will never understand the church's message of solidarity with the poor as long as they seek to hold on to their privileges. The gospel phrase "Even if the dead were to preach to them" fully applies to them. We must pray constantly for their conversion. *(Letter to Inás L. V., July 17, 1979)*

Pastor

With my new hierarchical responsibility, I begin with this Lent my Way of the Cross. In spite of my human weakness, I take strength in the sure hope of sharing also in the Resurrection of the Lord. *(Letter to Miguel O. P., March 23, 1977)*

I think that the Lord has wanted my ministry as archbishop to begin in this Lent as a road to Calvary in order to show forth the hope of an archdiocese with greater unity and greater faith. *(Letter to Monseñor José L. S., March 28, 1977)*

You may have read in the press that this new responsibility has begun with a road to Calvary, despite which and by the grace of God I am moving on with a faith that only the Lord can enlarge and with the joyful hope that a new life has begun in this archdiocese, with a clergy almost totally united with their bishop in these difficult times. *(Letter to Mons. Alfonso Lopez Trujillo, March 23, 1977)*

Your words, brief but greatly encouraging to my work as a bishop facing a humanly speaking difficult situation, but illumined by the light of your words of friendship, help me meditate on the Great and Eternal Priest who changes pain to joy and death to resurrection. *(Letter to Juan E. B., April 2, 1977)*

Your encouraging words coming from a brother priest who, for a long time, lived with us in our reality through the mission of the church, strengthen my spirit as bishop in a situation that is cloudy but that itself illuminates the great truth that Christ's work continued through his church is beyond persecution, weapons, and death.

I thank the Lord that, thanks to your prayers and those of our brothers, I have been able to maintain great serenity in order to make the decisions required. *(Letter to Fr. Juan D., March 24, 1977)*

The first fruits of my time as archbishop have included a crisis. The goodness of the Lord has helped us bear up under it with interior joy, and it has given us an archdiocese which is a true community of faith, characterized by a unity among the clergy never seen before, and a people close to their humble pastor, all of them with a deep pride at feeling committed to the mission God has given the church at this current moment. *(Letter to Fr. Guillermo D., March 24, 1977)*

Now it has fallen to you to strengthen the faith and spirit of this brother, friend, and companion of yours, and to do that with verses that are truly inspired, and bring serenity, and have a gospel content. They make me meditate on the beyond, which all pastors must contemplate with fixed gaze, to ensure that their pastoral work is faithful to the desires of Christ, without fearing the storms that make the church more beautiful. *(Letter to Fr. Baltasar G. M., March 30, 1977)*

In a Sinful Society

Our people, and those of most Latin American countries, are living in very difficult situations. Injustice and violence are present at every moment, and their fundamental rights are frequently violated. I beg you to keep us in your prayers. We need them. My role as pastor is very difficult, but the Lord is giving us grace as I try to fulfill it in the most evangelical way possible. *(Letter to Cistercian monks of Rohan, April 18, 1979)*

Thank you for your encouraging words about my Sunday homilies. I see it as part of my role as pastor to cleanse our people's history of so much sin, so much injustice and violation of the rights of the humble. Christ is walking this road with us, and wants us to arrive at the fullness of history having developed his love and his peace based on the justice of his gospel. *(Letter to Rogelio M. S., October 10, 1979)*

For a pastor it's encouraging to know that Christians are able to understand the illuminating word of the Lord. Thank you very much for your prayers and for the affection reflected in your letter. I, in turn, pray to the Lord that, as the Good Shepherd to his flock, he will protect them in these difficult moments from being led astray by the media, which are so rigged and commercialized. *(Letter to Juana de H., October 31, 1977)*

With the Spirit of Faith

I thank you for your interest in our church, and especially its priests, making a good appearance before the world. I invite you to stay united to the Pastor of this archdiocese in the same faith, hope, and love.

We try to maintain an evangelical position in this concrete reality. It has been misinterpreted by many who still do not see it as being for their brothers and sisters. Let us pray for them, that the Lord will touch their hearts; and may we all strive to live God's reign in this world. We will always encounter contradiction, and when we do we will see it as a sign of fidelity to God and his people. *(Letter to Angela Maria de P., November 22, 1979)*

Thank you for your letter and your wish for Jesus Christ to be in my heart. This connects with the dearest wish of a pastor, since Jesus is the author of justice and peace. Let us join in the prayer he taught us, asking "thy kingdom come," a kingdom of justice, peace, and love. *(Letter to Aun Joseph C., December 4, 1979)*

Let us always carry on with our mission as church to teach and preach, and to be a channel of grace to reconcile God with men and women, and men and women with each other. *(Letter to Fr. Astor R., November 16, 1979)*

With Humility

I ask the Lord to give me the humility necessary to recognize any error that I may have committed with this "new kingdom" that is fermenting among our people through your organization. I also ask Him to give me the courage necessary to change any mistaken position I may have taken, perhaps not out of bad will but for not having had sufficient clarity. My fundamental desire is to be with the flock that the Lord has entrusted to me. (*Letter to Astor R., November 16, 1979*)

I'm very grateful to you for your letter of solidarity and support for my mission as pastor of this archdiocese in the face of continuous calumnies from people who are ill-intentioned or ignorant. I congratulate you on your ecclesial and Christian spirit.

From the moment when I took over as archbishop, I have understood that I am not alone. The Lord has entrusted me with this job, and he is giving me his grace continually, and I have felt as well the support of the people of God. (*Letter to José Raúl O., March 29, 1978*)

As pastor I'm happy to see that lay Christians feel that the church is theirs, and are concerned that people not lose the faith. (*Letter to the neighbors of San José Villanueva, October 27, 1977*)

In my difficult mission I am strongly encouraged by your sincere support, especially because you have found in my words the thinking and heart of a priest who is open to the church's magisterium as represented by the Pope. *(Letter to Pedro Juan G., July 17, 1979)*

Even to Die with Christ

I'm very happy that you understand that the church can be effective in its evangelizing role only when there is perfect communion between the communities and their bishop. I suggest that we stay closely united by praying for each other. *(Letter to José Saúl G., December 3, 1979)*

It is true that the Salvadoran church, and especially the archdiocese, is at a difficult moment. There is no doubt that, for those who truly commit themselves to the gospel, this implies participating, in their own suffering, in the pain that Christ suffered as part of delivering his message of liberation. But in Christ there is no pain without hope, and no sadness that will not be converted to joy. We can best encourage each other by praying for one another. That will be the source of our faithful action. *(Letter to Fr. Antonio A., July 25, 1979)*

I am very grateful for your interesting letters, which reflect your own prayer and sacrifice. They do me great good, helping me to serve better as pastor. There is no doubt that your testimony of suffering, united with the pain of Christ on the cross, is a hopeful sign of liberation for so many members of the people of God who need the spiritual support of their brothers and sisters at this time. *(Letter to Guadalupe de Jesús, July 17, 1979)*

Let us walk the road together, looking toward Christ and trying to be witnesses of the Christ who lived, loved, and worked as a man among the dispossessed. He knows their needs and hopes. I praise your words of support, in closing ranks with your bishop to form one solid voice, one arm to struggle for integral liberation based on evangelical love.

To strengthen this process of seeking justice—which we should be doing all day, every day—let our prayers for each other be our source of strength and fidelity. *(Letter to the Christian community of Soyapango, September 5, 1979)*

Carry on, always seeking truth, justice, peace, and freedom. Christ will give us strength so that we won't lose heart along the way. True evangelization is the only path to integral liberation. *(Letter to the Christian community of Caserío de la Joya, June 7, 1979)*

You should try, more and more, to find and live gospel values. God is with his people in their struggle to achieve their freedom. Let us draw near to him and hear his word, which saves and frees. Be firm in your faith; encourage each other and never lose hope.

Grace is greater than sin, and light is greater than darkness. Some day they will triumph. The risen Christ is our hope. *(Letter to the Christian community of Cerro Grande, June 7, 1979)*

I recognize and respect the work of the Sisters in Arcatao. I myself have seen the fruits of their work in that rural zone. It is one of the most repressed areas of the countryside, but thanks to God, and despite the persecution, it is alive as a community, and becoming more conscious and more dynamic as a result of its contact with the gospel and with Christ the Liberator.

I believe that pastoral work that's truly committed to the poor will be always be persecuted; perhaps the persecution is a sign that the church, in its prophetic mission, is being faithful to the Lord in the midst of his people. *(Letter to the Daughters of Mary Immaculate de G., September 20, 1979)*

The road of the evangelizer is hard, and only the brave count. The gospels predicted trials like theirs for those who work with the Lord, and only those who persevere will triumph. *(Letter to Cruz O., June 18, 1977)*

Your voice and many others greatly encourage me in my work of preaching the good news to the poor and to the rich who, if they truly convert, will seek to live and feel like the poor. *(Letter to Rafael Humberto P., November 17, 1978)*

Priest

For your information, I am the new archbishop of San Salvador. I have found that the clergy here are very responsible and hard-working and most are in the line of Vatican II and Medellín. Above all, they are united to their pastor in their love of God and their neighbor, and for those most despised and vilely trampled upon by an inhuman system and by authorities who are at the service of minorities. *(Letter to Fr. Luis María H., July 11, 1977)*

Priests are chosen from among us and placed among people to free them physically and spiritually. Because they are children of God and a sublime image of God, all people deserve a life of dignity. The priest's mission is to help build, for all of God's children, a Kingdom of Justice which God wants to shine here on earth as a sign of that ultimate justice which we will enjoy in heaven. In justice, the peace and love of God kiss. *(Letter to Esther G., April 25, 1979)*

We need priests in our church, priests who are committed to God in service to their people. Given the interest you tell me you're feeling, it may be that the Lord is calling you to serve him in this way.

A vocation to the priesthood is God's call to a man to orient and direct himself to his people in the different Christian communities. It would be good if you began to participate in the Christian community in your parish. *(Letter to José E. R., October 25, 1977)*

This is a transcendent step in your life of service to the church. Prepare yourself with good spiritual exercises, and read the Bible—becoming steeped in it. In his letter to Timothy, St. Paul has some good advice for deacons. *(Letter to Ezequiel G., June 2, 1978)*

Put all your efforts into preparing yourself for a fruitful priesthood. We need priests with open minds and big hearts, ready to serve and love God, the church, and their people. *(Letter to Ezequiel G., September 27, 1978)*

What you say in your letter gives me new hope in my mission of following the path laid out for us by the eternal teacher, Jesus Christ, who took on our flesh to bring us to the Father. We are the prolongation of this mystery of Christ. Father Neto[1] took seriously this mission of the Christian, of the priest. *(Letter to Fr. Luis V. de V., December 21, 1978)*

Our mission is difficult, but the Lord is with us, and that gives us strength to continue proclaiming his message. We have hope in our clergy and in the women religious who, more and more, are responding to the church's call, and in the laypeople who take seriously their commitment to the gospel and the church.

Pray to the Lord that his word will be clear and proper for us to proclaim it to the people. *(Letter to Fr. Baltasar G. M., November 7, 1977)*

Our archdiocese needs priests who will give themselves completely to the service of the church and the people, who will be light and yeast and witnesses to

---

[1] *Editor's note:* Ernesto Barrera, known as "Neto," was a priest of the archdiocese. He was killed by the National Guard on November 28, 1978.

Christ among the people. *(Letter to Fr. Juan S., September 14, 1978)*

More and more the cross is a reality in our Latin America. Our job is to bear it and give it its true sense, so that the sufferings and struggles of our people can be united with the redeeming cross of Christ. *(Letter to Fr. Pablo G., March 21, 1979)*

In these recent years some of our priests have gone to the presence of the Father. Here on earth their blood nourishes the seeds that some day will grow into robust trees giving testimony to the gospel. This has to confound those who adore power and money, and are incapable of understanding the language of the church. *(Letter to Guillermo N., July 23, 1979)*

Last June 20 the White Warriors Union murdered Fr. Rafael Palacios. Once again our archdiocese is watered in the blood of one of our beloved priests. Rafael did excellent work forming grassroots Christian communities. We had great hopes for him. He was murdered near the church of El Calvario in Santa Tecla, and was buried in Suchitoto. His fidelity in the midst of so much misunderstanding, his perseverance and responsibility in the daily pastoral work, and the seriousness with which he took his commitment to the priesthood: these are the great challenges he leaves with us priests. He was a man who lived what he preached. *(Letter to Fr. Astor R. April 7, 1979)*

Let us carry on, with all of us of one mind and one heart with the church, attentive to the cries of the poor and illuminating our actions with the light of the Gospel. *(Letter to Fr. José R. V., October 9, 1978)*

I believe that if we—clergy and bishop—have as our goal action by the church that never loses track of our evangelical vocation, we will have to eliminate extremism, unsuitable methods, and, especially, egotisms which complicate even further the crisis we're confronting, and which, of course, destroy unity. *(Letter to Fr. José de C. P., July 27, 1977)*

I earnestly beg you not to take part in the demonstration which student groups and unions are preparing for August 30. You're well aware of the problems that our church is confronting at this historic moment. The participation of priests in demonstrations of this kind would only add more problems, and so would not be right or advisable. We've had more than enough bitter experience with this kind of thing. *(Letter to Fr. José C. R., August 27, 1977)*

It's unfortunate that those who should be aligned with the advanced pastoral positions of Medellín and Puebla[2] instead opt for a comfortable position that leaves them indifferent to the needy ones the gospel speaks of.

---

[2] *Editor's note:* Reference to the assemblies of the Latin American Bishops in Medellín, Colombia, in 1968 and in Puebla, Mexico, 1979, which charted the church's "preferential option for the poor."

Let us pray that we will be able to persevere, and that many others will return to a faithful position. *(Letter to Antonio R. N., August 24, 1979)*

I thank you for the work you've done for the archdiocese all your life. The Lord will give you back that and more, will give you all that you deserve. I know about your sufferings during the church's aggiornamento, and about your good will toward your parishioners. We will miss you greatly. May God our Father guide all your steps and keep you in his service. *(Letter to Fr. Manuel B., December 8, 1978)*

I'm sorry that your parish work kept you from joining the priests in your vicariate at the retreat. A period of meditation is always good, but doing it with others helps to illuminate, unify, and strengthen the pastoral reality. I hope that in the future, the dates chosen for the retreats will fit with your pastoral work in the parish. *(Letter to Fr. Salvador I., November 27, 1979)*

I thank you again for your solidarity with the pastoral plan of the archdiocese, a solidarity that has led you to raise your voice to protest the lack of communication; nevertheless, I want to remind you of the serenity of the truth, so that you won't unnecessarily expose yourself to conflicts; but if it's necessary to be courageous, you will have to follow your own conscience. *(Letter to Fr. Cataldo P., November 8, 1979)*

The Laity

I feel very happy when I see many laypeople living with
Christian ideals and persevering in the struggle to be
faithful to the gospel despite persecution. Christ was the
first to be persecuted for living with the ideal of serving
and freeing humanity; he even gave his own life. Our
struggle is not in vain. The Lord makes it very clear in
Matthew 25: "For I was hungry and you gave me food;
I was thirsty, and you gave me drink."

Also, in John's Gospel (15:18–27), Jesus speaks about
the hatred the world had for him and has for us Christians.
Also Matthew chapter 10, John 16, and in the Acts of the
Apostles. *(Letter to Antonio Cruz D., March 15, 1978)*

Since you've asked me what I think about the formation people get in military barracks, I'll answer in terms
of the reality that we see every day in our country.

To be sure, in a barracks they don't teach you how
to live according to God's plan. You know what's been
done here by many people who were trained in barracks.
You can see clearly that theirs weren't Christian actions.
To be a human being is to have the courage to build a
world of fellowship, and to take on the social and personal
problems that come up every day; that is, to fulfill the task
for which God has put us on this earth. To be a human
being is to build, not to destroy. If it turns out that they
do draft you and you end up in a barracks, always be true

to your Christian principles, and be brave in defending them. *(Letter to José Heriberto S. R., November 16, 1977)*

In the sacrament of confirmation we commit ourselves to be "soldiers of Christ"—that is, to struggle against the sin that reigns in our society and in ourselves, and to suffer in that struggle. We must be aware of the obligation we have, as children of God, to build a more human and just society, in which we all see and love each other as brothers and sisters. *(Letter to Adelita S. G., November 16, 1977)*

I thank you and praise you for your interest in the farm workers, which I hope is sincere. What I would like to ask you is, what do you mean by "true gospel"? Because it could be that you understand what some seek, which is "not to awaken the consciousness of the farm workers, but to keep taking advantage of them."

The Gospel of St. Luke, 4:18ff., is very interesting, particularly where it says, "The spirit of the Lord is upon me, for he has anointed me to bring the good news to the afflicted. He has sent me to proclaim liberty to captives, sight to the blind, to let the oppressed go free." It's a profound theme, one that's worth meditating on, sincerely and without any egotism.

We recall from the church's magisterium the words of Paul VI to the farm workers in Colombia in 1968: "I know of the cries of protest that are stifled in your throats in the face of so much misery, oppression, and injustice. . . . The Church will speak on your behalf." I recommend that you read the Medellín Document and the many messages of John Paul II calling for respect for the sacred rights of the poorest, and the Document of Puebla, No. 144, which says that the church should act independently of temporal powers, in order to avoid any interference in its mission. *(Letter to Eugenio A., July 18, 1979)*

I have the same opinion as you do about the applause in the cathedral. I believe people do that as a way of showing their gratitude to the church for being the only voice denouncing the injustices that are being committed here. *(Letter to María Leonor D., August 23, 1979)*

Adhering to the Magisterium

My visit to Rome was a quick one. The archdiocese's desire to live out Vatican II and Medellín has led my brothers in power to visit much persecution and violence on my other brothers, the dispossessed. The anguished cry of a people hungry for everything has now reached the throne of God. *(Letter to J.L.G., June 29, 1977)*

Colonel, I have received a copy of your article "Politicians or Pastors?" Thank you for sending it to me. I feel that I have a pastoral duty to offer some clarifications about its content.

In my second pastoral letter of August of 1977, I analyzed some points about the mission of the church in our times, in the face of the sinful reality that we are

living in our country. The same is true for the church in
Latin America.

There has been nothing of hate or vengeance in the
church's actions. We simply want to recall that great truth
of Jesus: what love wants is to truly humanize all men
and women, and toward that end it seeks efficient ways
to return the humanity of those who have lost it. The love
the church is preaching has as its model the love of Jesus:
"Love one another, as I have loved you." His love wasn't
just sentimental or abstract; it was gratuitous and efficient,
and it led him to lay down his life. He wanted men and
women to be converted. He had relationships with some rich
people, but it was in order to convert them; for example,
Zacchaeus gave half of his possessions to the poor, and said
that if he had defrauded anyone of anything, he would give
them back four times as much. Jesus defended the rights
of the poor, and showed them the way to regain their lost
dignity. The church has not called on people to rise up
against one another, but it has invoked two main points:
First, what Medellín says about institutionalized violence
(section on Peace, 16). When there exists a situation of
permanent and structural injustice, that situation itself is
violent. And second, the church realizes that in this situation, anything it says may sound violent, even though it is
guided by love. Its struggle against egotism itself, against
the inertia that is more inclined to dominate than to serve,
and against the violence of the current situation.

Another way of accusing the church of being unfaithful is to call it Marxist. When the church recalls the most elemental rights of men and women, and puts all of its institutional and prophetic power at the service of the weak and dispossessed, some try to label that Marxist. The church has always defended the fundamental rights of people to their material goods. What moves the church is an ethical interest, grounded in the faith. The church isn't interested in any ideology as such, and should be ready to speak critically if any ideology, socialist or capitalist, is absolutized. The current capitalist system is also practical materialism.

The church, like Christ, is interested in all people and in the whole person. That's why the church in Latin America has spoken out in defense of human rights, which are being continuously violated. To grasp the severity of the misery and oppression suffered by our farm workers, all you need to do is visit the countryside. It is said that the same is true for factory workers.

There is no freedom of expression; if someone asks for a piece of bread, he's thrown in jail. It's forbidden to say that people are dying of hunger and malnutrition, that they have no health care, that the unemployment rate is very high (65 percent in our country), and that illiteracy is a serious problem.

Christ came to the whole person, body and soul; his mission was integral. That's why the church's message and actions have strong repercussions in society, and which could be seen as "political." The church has the right and the obligation to speak about the political order "when the fundamental rights of a person or the salvation of souls require it. In this, she should make use of all the means—but only those—which accord with the gospel and which correspond to the general good according to the diversity of times and circumstances." (Vatican II, *Gaudium et Spes* 76)

The church's social teaching has a strong biblical base. Anyone who reads the Bible without letting their passions or ego get in the way can see that. As St. John says in one of his letters, "Anyone who says 'I love God' and hates his brother, is a liar, since whoever does not love the brother whom he can see cannot love God whom he has not seen."

What does it mean to love one's brother or sister in Latin America? *(Letter to Col. Romeo B.R., June 30, 1978)*

I have received your letter about the difficulties you have faced in your pastoral work since the birth of your grassroots Christian community, because of the rejection of your parish priest.

I understand your situation and your concerns. Don't get discouraged in the face of these problems. Go forward in the daily work of building a church which is ever more faithful to the gospel in the context of the reality our people are living. If you follow the pastoral plan of the archdiocese, you will have my support.

Medellín and Puebla have given great importance to the formation and growth of grassroots Christian communities. So has our archdiocese. We are at a difficult stage. The changes have only barely been grasped by those who still haven't taken seriously the responsibility that every Christian, whether priest, religious, layperson, or bishop, has in the building of the Kingdom of God, which begins here on earth and will reach its fullness at the end of time. *(Letter to George A., July 5, 1979)*

You're right in what you say about deficiencies in the administration of justice in this country. That leads us, as church, to be constantly calling the new government authorities and the different sectors of society to form a clear vision of our national reality that will allow them to find ways to bring justice and freedom to the Salvadoran people in the light of the gospel and the church's magisterium. *(Letter to Fr. Santiago G., October 26, 1979)*

Your situation grieves me, and I know that there are many brothers and sisters who, like you, don't have the basic necessities of life. I hope the Lord will help all Salvadorans do their part in the building of justice by living the Christian values of justice and love. *(Letter to Marcelino de J. M., November 9, 1979)*

God has created the earth with love, so that all his children can enjoy its fruits. What we need in the country is an agrarian reform program based on social justice, and that would benefit all of the farm workers. *(Letter to Guillermo N., December 22, 1979)*

We need to decide if we're going to settle for resting in our own peace, or if we think that peace is a universal gift, and something that all of our brothers and sisters have a right to. The firm basis for peace is justice, meaning that everyone would live with the dignity they deserve as human beings and children of God, and not a situation in which a few have a great deal, and many have so little that they can barely live as human beings. Let us ask Christ for the necessary strength to walk the road of justice that leads to peace. *(Letter to Manuel M. C., October 10, 1979)*

We trust that Christ, the first advocate of a more just and fraternal society, will, through his church, let shine the truth that frees and dignifies human beings, destroying the cunning and inhuman means used by those who dominate to subjugate their victims. *(Letter to Ego S., November 20, 1978)*

Carry on building the Kingdom of God, and remember that for there to be a new society you must become the "new men and women" St. Paul speaks of. Study the gospels and the documents of the church and your bishop. They will help you act firmly and be very conscious of what you're seeking.

Don't allow difficulties to defeat you. There's a great deal of strength in you young people, and if it's nourished by the presence of Jesus, it can be something very positive for building the new society that we seek, and which we call the Kingdom of God. *(Letter to an apostolic group in Chalatenango, November 9, 1979)*

How wonderful it is when brothers and sisters work together. That provides strength. And if you're working to build a more just and human world, God will bless you abundantly. May all of you brothers and sisters be light for your friends and neighbors. Hopefully some day your way of the cross, the road to Calvary, will turn out to be the road to Resurrection. *(Letter to José Eulalio A., August 1, 1977)*

Let the goal of our work as Christians be to ask the Lord that we might unite all men and women in one family before Christ, based in justice and liberty. *(Letter to María Elena M., July 29, 1979)*

All of us who are preaching the truth of the gospel will suffer what Christ suffered. As St. John said in his gospel, the darkness can't bear the light, and so tries to extinguish it. It pains me to see so many Catholics who are that in name only, and who are capable of betraying their own brothers and sisters. Let us pray for their conversion. Even Jesus wasn't able to free himself from such people; he had a Judas in his group.

The fruit of your prayers is obvious: it's only through the abundant grace of the Lord that I've been able to feel such moral strength. Whenever possible I'll go to that holy house for a rich exchange of impressions and an experience of inner renovation. Meanwhile, I trust that we will find ourselves united every day in prayer, the sure source of nourishment for our service to the Lord, an exercise of our love for him and his church. *(Letter to Fr. Segundo A., June 1, 1977)*

Let us stay close in prayer, so that the light of the Lord will be intensified in the great work of building his

kingdom and so that, in our pilgrimage, we will have
the Christian hope which transforms difficulties into joy.
(Letter to Raul A. H., September 21, 1977)

I'm happy that we're united in prayer, for it's the
source of the hope that keeps us in sufficient balance in
order to analyze all difficulties in serenity. *(Letter to Fr.
Luis Maria B., March 3, 1977)*

Let us pray together so that Christ the Eternal Priest
will help the archdiocesan clergy to do pastoral work that
will never stray from our evangelical vocation. *(Letter to
Fr. Matteo Q., April 2, 1977)*

All of us in the church have a very important mission.
We each do what we can, according to our capabilities.
Prayer is very important. Those of us who are in constant
activity need it, and we need your prayers, too. *(Letter to
Tomas R., March 31, 1978)*

I want to take this opportunity to send you a brief
message: it's the strength of the gospel that keeps you
united, looking out for each other's needs, sharing not
only the little we have but our living faith, so that, seeing
you and hearing you, those who are a bit discouraged
will be able to catch their breath and then continue in
the following of Christ, which at this time is very difficult, but it is that very difficulty that will prove your
faith. Hate no one, no matter how great the evil they
have done to the community. Instead, pray for them,

that they may be converted, open their eyes, and find the truth. *(Letter to the Christian community of Arcatao, November 2, 1979)*

Christ, the Eternal Priest, keeps us united through prayer, the soul of every apostolate. *(Letter to Bishop Bruno T., March 30, 1977)*

Take heart, Father. Let us carry on in faith, hope, and love. We're not alone; the Lord is with us and always will be. Let us, together, be of one mind and one heart with the church, steady in our role as pastors. *(Letter to Fr. Antonio A., December 6, 1977)*

To Be of One Heart and Mind with the Church[3]

As committed Christians, you can, on the basis of your faith, illuminate your just political struggles and demands,

---

[3] *Editor's note:* "Sentir con la Iglesia" was the episcopal motto that Romero chose when he was named bishop. It is typically translated as "thinking with the church," though the Spanish word *sentir* has the double meaning of *thinking* and *feeling*. When he originally chose this motto, it is likely that Romero understood this more in terms of adherence to orthodoxy, as in "thinking with the church (as *magisterium*)." It seems that his understanding grew more in the direction of "thinking *and feeling* with the church (as *the people*)." Here we have translated this as "being of one heart and mind with the church." Elsewhere, we will use the original Spanish phrase.

but always caring for your maximum treasure, which is your faith. Our fidelity to that faith is service in love. May it be strengthened by mutual prayer. *(Letter to a Christian community, September 13, 1979)*

I congratulate you for understanding that our ecclesial mission is to announce the transcendent liberation of the people, not with hatred or violence, but with love. May mutual prayer strengthen in us the great gospel values. *(Letter to Victor C. R., December 3, 1979)*

I always remember you with great affection for giving yourself so generously to the cause of the church in its mission of offering people not only an imminent but also a transcendent liberation leading to the definitive encounter with Christ. *(Letter to Rudy S., December 4, 1979)*

Carry on, guided by the light left you by Fr. Palacios, his irreproachable life, his love of the Kingdom of God, made concrete in addressing the needs of our people. You are the seeds of the Kingdom; he was attentive in taking care of you. *(Letter to the grassroots Christian community of Santa Tecla, October 2, 1979)*

We who try to follow the gospel of Jesus are hated, but that is natural; the darkness can't bear the light. Jesus was and continues to be a stumbling block for many. Don't be discouraged by the fact that we're being persecuted. See it as a sign that, in reality, we are trying to build the

Kingdom of God. *(Letter to the grassroots Christian community of San Cristobal, June 7, 1978)*

Carry on, living the gospel more and more, living that fraternal spirituality that was so characteristic of the first Christian community. The grassroots Christian communities are a hope for evangelization in Latin America. May they be a leaven of unity, love, peace, justice, and good relations among all. *(Letter to the pastoral team of Ilopango, April 26, 1978)*

Let us have courage and do what we can, whether it be a lot or a little, for the good of our brothers and sisters, especially the most needy. Let us take our Christian commitment ever more seriously, taking up the plow that has been left unattended by all of the priests and catechists who've been killed in recent years. *(Letter to Miriam B., July 13, 1979)*

I congratulate you for your brave Christian testimony in spite of all the threats and taunts. Let our fidelity to Christ be the best answer to those who scorn and persecute the church. Let us stay united in prayer. *(Letter to the Christian community of Cinquera, December 5, 1978)*

Though the cause of Christ may be betrayed by those who ought to be serving it, we should stay faithful. Christ showed us the path of justice, peace, and truth. We should take that path along with our brothers and sisters, without paying attention to the threats, calumnies, and persecution by those who adore money and brute force. Praying for each other will give us strength. *(Letter to José A. A., July 29, 1979)*

I'm glad you understand that the church is stronger when, humanly speaking, it is weakest. Christ guides it and strengthens it so that it can carry out its mission permanently. *(Letters to the catechists of Comalapa, September 10, 1979)*

Let us continue in the daily struggle to extend the Lord's message to all people. All of us—priests, laypeople, religious women and bishops—have this duty. To be of one mind and one heart with the church [*Sentir con la Iglesia*] is also to be one mind and heart with Christ. To think and feel [*sentir*] with our suffering people is to think and feel [*sentir*] with the church which makes its own the sorrows, the joys, and the hopes of the men and women of our time. *(Letter to Inocenta R., April 12, 1978)*

The pastoral work of the women religious in the parishes encourages me in my mission as pastor. Carry on, always being of one mind and one heart with the church and the people [*sentir con la Iglesia y con el pueblo*]. We must serve them according to the norms of the gospel. *(Letter to Sr. Marcelina P., August 8, 1978)*

Part II

ADVICE

෴

The concept of the priest as minister, that is, the minister who distributes God's grace and celebrates the mysteries of our salvation, is fundamental in the thought of Monseñor Romero. But during his ministry as archbishop the predominant concept was of the priest as proclaimer of the gospel, as "the man who directs and guides his people." Monseñor Romero writes constantly of the three dimensions of priestly service or ministry: "servant of the Lord, of the church, and of his people."

To be a servant of the Lord is to be a witness to Him and His gospel—not to any other doctrine or ideology belonging to this world. As St. Paul writes, there are some who preach another gospel that is not that of the Lord Jesus. Or as Monseñor Romero himself expresses in one of his letters, "so that our people's sufferings may be united

47

*to those of Jesus on the cross, and they may thus discover
the true meaning of their suffering."*

*To be a servant of the church is to extend the grace of
God's kingdom in the world. Monseñor Romero speaks
in one of his letters about the requirement that the priest
"never turns the light away from his gospel vocation." So
he must avoid becoming a politico, he must not allow his
ministry to be bought by the powers of this world, and
must by no means be suborned by the gifts and privileges
that the powerful try to offer him.*

*Referring to his ministry as a pastor, Monseñor
expressed with limpid clarity in one of his letters that
to be a servant of his people is to "cleanse the history of
our people from so many sins of injustice and violations
of the rights of the poorest and bring them with Christ
to the fulfilment of history."*

*It is admirable how, after having been a priest almost
totally focused on the liturgy, or to put it in biblical terms,
after having been a Temple priest, Monseñor Romero
became a street priest, a Tres Calles priest,[1] where he
heard the cries and groans of the poor and the wounded
and defenseles who were victims of the violence of the
powerful.*

*The gospel of Luke (10:29-37) contains the parable
of the "Good Samaritan." In the bible of Monseñor's life*

---

[1] In the *Tres Calles* [Three Streets] incident on June 22,
1975, the National Guard murdered five peasants. Romero went
to comfort the victims' families and say Mass for the victims.

that parable has changed its name. In Monseñor Romero's life it is called the "Good Priest." Because when the priest went off with clean hands to get to the Temple in time, Monseñor Romero stopped, heard the groans of someone at the point of death, and healed him with the voice of hope: "I have no silver or gold, but what I have I give you; in the name of Jesus Christ of Nazareth, stand up and walk" (Acts 3:6).

The "Good Samaritan" ceased to be just a parable and became reality. Monseñor Romero was converted by the poor; by those who were suffering, hungry and persecuted. And by God's word he helped them so that their hunger, suffering, persecution, and death, became the subject of the Beatitudes, rather than an engine of violence.

To Convert Our Lives and Existence into an Apostolate

On Not Living Isolated

I'm happy that many members of the community are being attended to by the parish priest in their Christian formation. Without doubt, some places won't receive all the attention necessary, but if the laypeople keep taking on their responsibility in the work of the church, they'll soon be better attended to.

Christianity can't be lived in isolation. It should be lived forming communities, which will be symbols of love, brotherhood, and sisterhood.

Many people find the church's new way of working to be strange. But daily we see it as necessary that the Word of God be known everywhere, so that our faith can be well grounded.

If you have the chance to participate in some of the Communities, do it. You'll see that they're not strange, or outside Catholicism. Do it and you'll find that you're discovering your faith more and more. *(Letter to Josefa M., November 13, 1978)*

On Practicing Discernment

I congratulate you for belonging to the Nazareth group, and for the growth in your faith which you've experienced there. Those groups do so much good for our Christian communities.

I invite you to discover, amid the tragic events in our country, the message of Christ who wants a Christian people free of all oppression and injustice.

Let us pray to the Lord for each other, so that we can all be capable of living an evangelical love with our brothers and sisters, in a continuous and generous service. *(Letter to María Angelina B., September 12, 1979)*

Don't worry about those who resist the call to faith in Christ, and who curse against his word of life. There are many places where it's still necessary to plant the seeds of God. Prayer is the best way to help them, so that the gifts of faith and grace will be given to them. *(Letter to María M. U., October 24, 1979)*

Without Hatred

As for those who persecute the church, instead of hating them, it's better to feel sorry for them and pray that they be converted. *(Letter to María Josefina J. R., April 27, 1979)*

Keeping Your Eyes on Christ

I think this is the decisive moment for you to strengthen your relationship with Christ. We are never closer to Christ than when, despite physical or moral suffering, we give ourselves to him, with this painful situation that we endure or feel. I'm sure that you are capable of carrying out this giving yourself to the Lord. The result of this self-giving will come from Christ, and you can be sure that he will not be outdone in generosity.

It may be that those who don't love you will appear to triumph, but you should know that the triumph of what is not right is not a lasting triumph. Besides, it's often the case that what people see as triumph, God sees as failure.

I congratulate you for your devotion to the holy rosary. Put your situation in the hands of the Blessed Mother, and she will act as a kind-hearted mother.

I appreciate your willingness to help out in my pastoral work. Surely an occasion will come in your life when, as one baptized, you will have to offer some service to the church.

Know that you are not alone in resolving your problem. Our faith says that the power of the Savior will be with you. *(Letter to Leonor P. V., April 28, 1979)*

To Be Light and Salt

I see that you're a person who's aware of what's going on with your closest work neighbors. Let this be a gift that will help you discover how you can be a good friend, having an influence for the just and the true in those around you.

To be a Christian is to be concerned for your neighbor and to be at the service of the others in search of what the gospel sees as the good. *(Letter to Pedro Pablo R., November 15, 1979)*

Although the circumstances seem adverse, I think that we can benefit a great deal if we discover in them the presence of Christ.

Wherever we're surrounded by people, Christ is present in them, and our faith should illuminate whatever service we offer, even if it's only a word of encouragement. Let us trust that the difficult moments will pass soon, and that from them we can learn a great deal about life, which will enable us to better help others later. *(Letter to Dalton O., September 10, 1979)*

Take heart. Try to live very united to those around you, and caring for those who are in greatest need. Let all who approach you receive consolation and friendship. Christian life means making brothers and sisters and friends along the way, as Jesus did, giving ever more of ourselves and serving them more and more.

To Walk Uphill

I'm happy to send you the New Testaments that you requested. Reflect on them together and make commitments for your daily lives. The gospel always challenges us to make a concrete commitment in life. *(Letter to Emma P., March 23, 1979)*

My most sincere and affectionate congratulations on entering religious life. During your formation, may your ideal be fidelity to evangelical love seen in the poor and bloodied face of the people of God. Journeying hand in hand with them toward their total liberation in Christ should fulfill every desire of our life. *(Letter to Edith I. C., September 10, 1979)*

The service of the Lord is difficult, uphill. But he provides the grace necessary for each and every one of us to fulfill the mission he has given us. To what mission will he call you? Will it be what has been born in your heart, a clear call from God?

It is important that you cultivate this call with great rectitude of soul, and with a life overflowing with love, peace, and truth. In your struggles, let these virtues shine, and let them cultivate in you this small seed that the Lord has entrusted to your life. *(Letter to Leonel A. M., August 1, 1977)*

Together with the work in the countryside, you should cultivate your spiritual gifts, your studies, your life itself so that little by little, and in accord with your own capacities, you can become a small builder of a more just world in which peace, love, and truth abound. *(Letter to Ricardo E. M., July 27, 1977)*

Seek the Face of Christ among the Poor

You have the capacity to love the Lord deeply. Love him with all your strength, and let this love overflow in favor of your brothers and sisters. This could be the most efficient weapon against the devil and his evils. *(Letter to Antonio P. E., August 11, 1977)*

It is exemplary to put all of our most difficult moments in God's care with complete trust. Faith is also trust. That's why it's important to seek solutions to our problems, but in the light of the word of Christ.

I ask you to pray much so that our people may grow in their faith, a faith that teaches us that God is reflected in every person, especially the poor and dispossessed. Let prayer be our first great step in faith, and let it help us be united in Christ. *(Letter to Julia S. de G., September 11, 1979)*

Reading your letter, I conclude that the paths of life, which may not seem clear to human eyes, are filled with light in God's eyes for those who accept him with serenity. Perhaps the circumstances of your life are more conducive today than they were before for knowing God and God's children. Surely your example of waiting with resignation serves as an example for many around you. *(Letter to Eleanora Ph., October 10, 1979)*

Word, Life, and Sacrament

I am very happy to send you the Bible you requested. Try to study it with respect and attention. The Word of God should be taken seriously and applied in our lives. In it you'll find the way to be happy in this world. In the gospels, Jesus shows us how the children of God should live. Try to read it frequently and share what you've learned there with friends, family, and neighbors. Ask your parish priest to help you. *(Letter to Doris E. L., March 27, 1979)*

Thank you for your note in which you say you find solace in seeing the church, through my person and my ministry, for looking after the Lord's most beloved: the poor. The Lord Jesus gives us a good example, since he was always ready to help the poor and the marginalized. That's why, brothers and sisters, I invite you as a Christian family to make the effort to be a true sign of the great family of the children of God, the church, whose mission is to serve our brothers and sisters. *(Letter to José R. L., September 18, 1979)*

More important than building the cathedral is building the church in each one of us. May all Christians form a true temple of adoration in the service of, and self-giving to, the others, especially the poor, following the example of Jesus, our elder brother. The cathedral is a symbol of unity, a call to form a church that is alive. *(Letter to Carmen F. G., March 22, 1979)*

Participation in the Mass

As for what you ask about listening to my homilies, I would say that if you're able to be present at the holy Mass in your parish, that is more important because the holy Mass demands a person's presence. In this case, if you want to listen to my homily, what you can do is pick an hour to attend Mass that is different from the time of the Sunday celebration in the cathedral. But if the two Masses are at the same time, you should know that part of my Sunday homily is rebroadcast on YSAX [the archdiocesan radio station] just before 6 a.m. on Monday morning.

I beg you to pray a great deal to the Lord for me, since only the strength that comes from prayer will provide the energy that's needed to guide the People of God in the right direction. *(Letter to Carlos A., April 27, 1979)*

I invite you to always stay united with Jesus in the Eucharist. This union will be seen if you are also united to the other people you relate to.

The first Eucharist was celebrated at the Last Supper that Jesus had with his apostles. On that day Jesus showed everyone how great was his love for us. He broke the bread as a sign of his giving himself to the others, of sharing. That is how he wants us to be: that we give ourselves over to serving others without expecting any reward. That is what we are committing ourselves to when we receive communion.

Whenever you receive communion, remember that you are making a commitment to serve the others with love. *(Letter to Ana Cecilia H., November 10, 1977)*

To Study the Word of God

I'm glad that you're continuing to participate in the Christian community. In it you will learn to live in communion with the local church, to share in the way shown to us in the Bible, to be of one mind and one heart with the church and the people, and to discover Christ, who calls us to follow him every day. *(Letter to David E. L. M., September 4, 1978)*

You have to decide whether the place where you are working helps you to live as a Christian or if it is a serious obstacle to being a Christian. Our norm must be the life of Jesus, and the two commandments he taught us: to love God and love our neighbor. If a job, no matter how well it pays, is an obstacle to living a Christian life, it will be necessary to leave it and look for another one.

Read the holy gospels. In them you will find the necessary strength and guidance for living a more authentically Christian life. *(Letter to Vicente C. R., July 11, 1978)*

To Turn to the Virgin Mary

Thank you very much for your kindness in sending me this scapular with your letter. I am even more grateful for your prayers, which, united with good works, will be precious in the eyes of the Lord.

I will use the scapular trusting in the protection of the Most Holy Virgin. Let me take this moment to say that when we use the scapular as one of the signs of our "popular devotion," it should not be accompanied by a superstitious faith, since God does not like superstition. Rather, we should use the scapular to express in a simple way our faith and trust in Divine Providence and in Mary's intercession. *(Letter to María Ofelia C. H., November 15, 1979)*

I praise your conscientious and persistent attitude of looking out for the well-being of the most humble members of our people.

As the coming of Christ, the greatest liberator, approaches, let us revive our faith and beg, in persevering prayer, that the country be saved from extremes, so that all of us Salvadorans can be faithful builders of Christ's kingdom. *(Letter to Pedro Pablo R., December 17, 1979)*

Solitude and Loneliness

I can see in your words that you are living a very unhappy life, closed in upon yourself. A person who does that cannot be happy, since the Lord has created us as people able to communicate with others who are made in his image and likeness. God never closes in on himself.

God gives himself to the others, and the greatest proof we have of this is that he gave his own Son for the salvation of the others. That is exactly what he wants us to do, too.

Christ's suffering didn't make him unhappy but, on the contrary, was the necessary step toward the resurrection—that is to say, toward life.

I would advise you to begin to reflect seriously on your life. God created you to be happy. You will not find that happiness by yourself, losing heart with your problems. You will find it to the extent that you discover that there are other people who suffer like you and who need you, so that together you can find a positive sense to your life.

God never wants anything bad for us, and God does not forget us and is always ready to forgive us and teach us how we should live. Read the gospel slowly and try to understand its words fully. Ask the Lord to give you light and draw near to people who can help you. Find out if your parish has Christian communities, and if it does, get involved in them. *(Letter to María, October 28, 1977)*

I believe that your great trust in the Lord is the best way to confront the current situation, since that trust, which is faith, gives us the conviction that God our Father knows and understands us, and accepts us as we are when he sees our desire to give ourselves to him.

Let your faith grow every day, and don't feel alone. Christ accompanies us and helps us with our difficulties, although for our own good he tests us for a while. *(Letter to Eleonor P. V., November 29, 1978)*

The Solitude That Enslaves

You have suffered quite a lot in your short life. Do not despair. You have to take advantage of the experiences you have had.

Often men aren't sincere, and are only trying to satisfy their instincts. Keep that in mind. In your case, you have distanced yourself from your parents who feel that you have deceived them, believing in a man who did not value you. Women can be strong and brave. Look at the Virgin

Mary, a young woman of your age. She is an example of a strong and brave woman who knew how to play her role and take on a great responsibility in her life.

It's never too late to start over. You can remake your life. Return to the side of your parents and follow their advice. One day you will find a man who really loves you and will form a Christian home with you. I recommend that you read the New Testament, where you will find the path to happiness. *(To L. P., February 15, 1978)*

I feel joy when I see that in many parts of our country there are Christians who have hope and are given over to the well-being of others.

I am happy to hear that the Word of God has reached the prison and has provided a glimmer of hope in the harshness of confinement. Continue helping to achieve the well-being of our brothers who are prisoners.

There are other prisons—for example, in the countryside—which are much worse. The gospel urges us to break the bonds of these prisons. Today there are prisons seemingly without bars, such as hunger, poverty, exploitation. Chapter 25 of St. Matthew's Gospel speaks of our responsibility as Christians in these situations. *(Letter to Carlos A. C., March 7, 1978)*

The Prayer That Frees

It pains me that you are in this sad situation. I will be very happy to help you financially so that you can get out on bail.

Don't get discouraged. The worst slavery is inner slavery; that's what greatly corrupts our life and the lives of others. That's the slavery that should concern us. Prison doesn't corrupt a person inside; time spent there should be taken advantage of, to reflect about our existence and whether it is in line with the will of God—that is, in service to others.

The gospel gives us great strength for living. I recommend that you read and reflect on it often. *(Letter to Dalton A. O., July 21, 1978)*

I see in your letter that you are visiting the prisons. I thank you for serving in this area, an area that I greatly love. I congratulate you for developing this great work of mercy. When I could, I always visited the prisoners.

The prayers of prisoners are very helpful and one should not lose sight of that. It's necessary to instill in them that if they bear their suffering with resignation, offering it up and uniting it with the suffering of Christ on the cross, they will be winning many graces for the church, and much good for society.

You can put the prisoners in contact with Christ through your words of hope and your presence, as often as possible. Jesus will reward you for having recognized him in one of these poor ones. *(Letter to María L. P., December 5, 1978)*

The Sickness That Revives Us

I advise you to take advantage of this time of illness to draw nearer to the Lord. Read the book of Job and the gospels. *(Letter to Saúl A. L., November 10, 1979)*

Offer up all your pain for those of us who are at the head of the church. Always be united with the Lord through prayer, and with the others through service. *(Letter to Carmen L., November 10, 1977)*

When we spend our lives loving God and the brothers and sisters whom God puts in our path, we don't await death with fear, but see it as a sure step to the house of the Father, where there will be no more inequalities, but all will be one in the Lord. *(Letter to Catalina A., March 16, 1979)*

Illness is a time we can take advantage of to reflect more deeply on our life and on what gives it meaning, as it also joins us to the sufferings of Christ for the salvation of so many, especially for the conversion of many. *(Letter to María M. U., August 16, 1979)*

Don't get discouraged. The Christian must be strong, must learn to hope against hope, mustn't give in, because although, humanly speaking, the situation may seem impossible, faith will help us discover possibilities which only the Lord can make real in us if with clear faith we present ourselves before him. *(Letter to Eleanora Ph., December 14, 1979)*

Wheat and Weeds

It is constant and honorable work that brings peace and overcomes difficulties. Continue on this path of honesty, as a Christian conscious of following the illuminating word of Jesus; and may your neighbors be attracted by your example. *(Letter to Juan Francisco R., October 30, 1979)*

Whenever I read in the gospel about the accompaniment and help that those devout women offered Jesus with such a great and pure love, I think that the Lord has continued inspiring other devout women in all times to continue, with a noble affection, accompanying and helping those who are shepherding his church.

It's a pity that today, as in the time of Jesus, there arise difficulties, divisions, rivalries, and ambitions for his kingdom. What you're telling me, with so much pain, about the members of the parish committee, pains me, too. But let's not settle for lamenting and remembering. Taking into account that there will always be wheat and weeds in the Church of Christ, let us follow the advice that he himself gave us for confronting evil: to have patience, waiting for the conversion of those who don't have faith nor work out of love, at the same time giving them a good example and praying for them.

I beg you not to leave the community definitively. If they won't let you do real work, there are many other things to do to build up the spirit of faith, hope, prayer, and reflection on the Word of God. Remember that the main thing is not the church building but the Christian spirit of the community. And although the building is necessary and God blesses those who do this work, more important is the pastoral work, which a priest can't do by himself; he needs help from those who have that Christian spirit. *(Letter to Adela de S., June 5, 1978)*

We see that in the gospel Jesus says to Nicodemus, "One must be born again through water and the Spirit in order to enter the kingdom of God." And St. Paul tells us to put off the old man and put on the new.

Here he's telling us to get rid of so many bad habits in our lives—for example, egoism, gossip, and other vices. Then what we should do is live Christian values: unity, love, justice, forgiveness, sharing, being kind to one another, attentive, and diligent. In this way we will be reborn, renewed interiorly, and making the change of life that the Lord asks of us. *(Letter to Paula M., November 9, 1979)*

Calumny is a grave evil, and unfortunately many people fall into this sin. Jesus himself, in his life, was constantly slandered, but he never took an attitude of retaliation, but rather kept silent when that was necessary. His response to slander was his life itself. They never found a sin in him; what they did see in him was a life of giving without limit, without egotistical interests, without ambitions. A simple, clean life; he was always friendly to everyone.

I advise you to read the Bible continually. That will be a big help for you in contemplating the life of Jesus.

Take heart! In this life there will always be those who, despite our good intentions, will see bad things which aren't there. What's important is that we be able to love even those who offend us, and forgive as Our Lord forgives us. *(Letter to María O. M., July 11, 1978)*

Conversion

I'm happy to see, in your letter, your concern that all Salvadorans really live in brotherhood and sisterhood. That is the concern of the entire church. That's why it proclaims that we should live according to the Word of God, and denounce all that opposes the divine plan. From this comes the call to conversion: to change our egotistical way of living and thinking, and put all of our capabilities at the service of others, especially the poorest. *(Letter to Pedro Pablo R., May 18, 1979)*

Not to Despair

Don't be discouraged. Crises are good, they help clarify the ideal and the depth of commitment to Christ. The important thing is to take advantage of everything that comes up in our lives, whether positive or negative. What's important is be ready to live the gospel with all the fidelity we're capable of, with authenticity. *(Letter to Sr. Socorro R., June 8, 1979)*

As for the favor you request, for me to speak with General Romero to ask him to help you economically, I don't think anything would come of that. I don't have the kind of friendship with him that would lead him to grant such a request. "Gold or silver have I none, but what I have I give you," said St. Paul to the invalid at the entrance to the temple. I'm sending you a check with this letter, which I hope will help you with your situation.

Try not to despair in the face of your problem. Don't let your nerves get the better of you. You'll find better solutions if you seek them with patience and calm. As for thinking about suicide, that will not improve the situation, and your children would suffer a great deal. Try to find a more economical living place and handle your finances better. Seek out your parish priest and talk about this with him. Don't let desperation win out. It's our own sin that brings us unhappiness. God wants us to be happy. He loves us and is always ready to forgive us. And when we begin to seek the Kingdom of God and his justice, all the rest will be added. Take heart! *(Letter to Milagro R., March 7, 1979)*

Don't Look Back

I say to you that Jesus invited us to look ahead, and not back. "No one who puts his hand to the plow and looks back is worthy of the kingdom of God."

God will take care of the past, no matter how bad it's been. He saved us with his blood. It's not a question of our merits, but of His. So, look ahead; what's behind is in God's hands. He loves you a great deal and He's counting on you for much. You can do a great deal of good. Look at your sins with humility. Go to confession and receive communion. Take on some apostolate. Courage, onward! Your parish priest can help guide you. *(Letter to Julio H., April 19, 1979)*

As for your problem, what I want to say to you is that God is our Father who loves us and, knowing us, also forgives us. What God sees is your conversion; that's what's important. So leave the past in God's hands.

The apostolic life and pastoral work that you're doing is already a good penance. Carry on, and remember that you don't have to tell anyone else about this, because now it's in God's hands. *(Letter to Felipa de Jesus H., March 30, 1979)*

Looking Ahead

It may be that, besides suffering, the road ahead will ask of us humility, patience, and more conversion on our part. But if it is the road to Jesus, we should not get discouraged, but rather live out our hope in our concrete lives, with faith in him who alone can totally satisfy all of our concerns. *(Letter to Oscar M., July 23, 1979)*

Start moving, and don't stop. The important thing is to get up and keep going. Along this new way, keep the Word of God ever present. It will give you the strength to continue with enthusiasm and fortitude, and it will show you the best way to go. If you come by the chancery office, I'll be glad to give you a Bible. *(Letter to Hector M., May 18, 1979)*

The important thing now is that you want to straighten out, and that's very powerful. Life isn't about declaring ourselves defeated. It's about evaluating where we had failings, and how to avoid them in the future.

First you should fortify yourself in virtue, value yourself as a Christian woman, and show those who have exaggerated your small faults that you're on the way to a Christian life which will be more serious and responsible; that you consciously want to be the architect of a destiny that will be the most dignified possible.

Don't pay any attention to what people say, and proceed toward your goal of being an exemplary wife who doesn't engage in casual relationships. *(Letter to Rosa, October 8, 1979)*

Marriage Counseling

I'm happy to see in your letter your great desire to live according to God's plan, which is to achieve true integral liberation of men and women. We have different kinds of limitations. Some could be called internal, such as egotism, hatred, hypocrisy, the sin which manifests itself in many ways; and the external limitations, such as ignorance, misery, and exploitation, etc.

But we, as true Christians, have the Good News of the gospel which is Jesus, the only one who can bring us to this complete liberation.

We Christians also have some efficient means—that is, the sacraments—which help us carry out the plan of God; in each of them we find a source of grace. For example, matrimony is the sacrament of God's call to men and women to be creators with him. They have to help their children, from a very young age, to grow in the image and likeness of God. That's why this sacrament is so important, since simply living together is not the same as living marriage as a mission entrusted by God. *(Letter to the Rodriguez family, November 9, 1979)*

Spouses Should Evangelize Each Other

Spouses have a difficult role in a marriage: to help each other reach fullness as persons and as Christians. It's not a task that's completed in a day, nor a week nor a year. It's a task for their entire lives, lived together.

If your husband isn't doing his job, you must—with patience and affection—help him see that and help him to change. But you don't have to let yourself be destroyed. If, after you've made every effort to bring peace and unity to the home, you see that it's going nowhere, you have a right to be happy because we, as children of God, have a right to happiness and freedom. *(Letter to Angelica, July 11, 1978)*

I hope your family situation has improved. The best response to people's gossip is the testimony of an exemplary life. As the mother of six children, you should stay faithful to the commitment you made at the altar. If your spouse is unfaithful, your life as a woman of dignity can help him recognize his errors and return to the home he abandoned. *(Letter to María Marta, November 13, 1978)*

Again I send you words of encouragement in your difficult relationship with your husband, a Mason and a nonbeliever. In the face of this difficulty, put your faith in God, and remember that for God nothing is impossible, and that just as St. Augustine's mother won for her son the grace of conversion, so too the Lord will not fail to hear and respond to your sufferings in this painful situation.

Try to discover in this situation a sign of our times, where the Lord asks us Christians to have a great fidelity of conscience and clarity of principles. These are the kinds of revelations the Lord is giving us now. They are difficult to understand and interpret. I think it is easier to be deceived by a revelation without suffering than by what you are going to discover in your concrete situation: the true liberty that God has given to men and women; and that if man is faithful to God, he will not prostrate himself before false idols, whatever they may be. It falls to you to discover what idol is most deeply rooted in your husband, so that with the help of God, he will also discover the love that God has for him. *(Letter to Angelica, December 14, 1979)*

Beyond Morality: Love

I received your letter, in which you expressed your doubts about what is permitted in marriage.

The conjugal act between legitimate spouses is not only licit but even meritorious before God, when the proper conditions exist. For the conjugal act to be licit, it must be done in a suitable way that will naturally produce offspring and promote greater love between the spouses.

When a spouse reasonably asks for the conjugal act, that request must be granted, both out of justice and to create a climate of greater union and love between the spouses. It should be kept in mind that the act should be by mutual agreement and with free consent, that both should be gentle and affectionate.

Human dignity and the sanctity of marriage demand this. This right should never be exercised only to satisfy passions or under poor physical and spiritual conditions. This act should be the culmination of the love lived between the spouses during the day.

There are no religious reasons that prohibit the conjugal act—for its being Lent or a feast day or for planning to receive communion. But if the spouses want to, they can, by mutual agreement, observe some days of abstinence to dedicate themselves to prayer. The preliminary and complementary acts accompanying the conjugal act are permitted as long as they are in accord with human dignity and promote love between the two of you.

Marriage is a sacrament in which both the husband and wife should manifest to others the love of Christ for his church, and anything that helps to promote that is permitted in marriage. *(Letter to Evangélica, March 6, 1979)*

Charity Begins at Home

Don't get discouraged. Frequently there are crises in marriages because men behave badly. Your own conduct will be the best reproach to him; always be attentive and affectionate with him and your children, and if it's possible, when there's a peaceful atmosphere, try to dialogue with him, not to argue but to help him see that his conduct is interfering with the happiness of your home. *(Letter to Lucinda, January 9, 1979)*

As for your family situation, I think the most advisable thing is for you to try not to lose your authority as head of the household, and not neglect those who live there. On the other hand, make your wife aware that anyone who might harm her or the children morally cannot be admitted to your home. Do what you can to dialogue with her when the atmosphere is peaceful. But the best thing would be for the two of you to speak with a priest you trust, in order to shed more light on your situation. *(Letter to José, January 10, 1979)*

As for the case you're asking me about, I would say the following: tell your husband that it is fine that he likes to read and hear the Word of God, but the important thing is to be a witness to it, to live in the way it tells us to live. The most important thing in the gospel is charity, and that has to begin at home, with the spouses treating each other with respect, being responsible about the needs of the home, and without abusing the concessions that marriage allows. Because more than being about sexual relations, conjugal life is about sharing hopes, plans, joys, sadness, failures, triumphs—in short, all the things that can happen in the life of your family. It also means thinking about the Christian education of your children, and trying to bequeath to them a trade, so that tomorrow they can take care of themselves. *(Letter to Adelina V., May 12, 1979)*

Witnesses to the Love of Christ

Keep in mind that as a Christian you should value the meaning of the special blessing the Lord grants all who elevate their conjugal union with the sacrament of matrimony. He gives these blessings so that you can always live one for the other; that is the fidelity of love.

God invites you to a special mission, wonderful and beautiful. To be co-creators with him, not just giving physical life to other beings, but also to take great care in forming them in the image and likeness of God. If you live this way in your marriage, you will be giving a great example to your community, because in this way you will be forming new men and women for a new society.

I'll also remind you of what I say to Christians in my third pastoral letter: you have a great duty to offer

witness and enlighten your political activity with your
faith. *(Letter to Miguel Angel L. G., November 6, 1979)*

To Defend Love and Life

I will tell you what I think with the same sincerity and
fidelity with which you ask for my opinion. As for the
impediment of kinship which exists in your case, the
church can give a dispensation, and I could do that myself
if in the end you decide to marry. But I can't, without
more information, recommend that you marry, given the
counter-indications you've pointed out.

As I mentioned, the problem of kinship can be overcome. You said you've had a surgery which, as I understand it, means you will not be able to have children. To
prevent problems later on, he should know this if you
decide to marry.

Experience tells us that the significant age difference,
with you being ten years older than him, might be a serious risk.

The fact that your boyfriend has had two children
with another woman is also something to think about.

I will pray that the Lord give you light in such a serious situation so that you will be able to act wisely, giving
thought to having a stable and Christian home. *(Letter
to Maria Celia, April 12, 1978)*

You don't say if you've had only a civil wedding, or
a church one, too. A marriage can't be dissolved easily,

but the sad reality is that most married people don't live the fullness of marriage.

Now that you've found someone to share your life with, try to live out what marriage really means. From your letter, I can see that that's what you want to do.

In a true marriage there should be fidelity, harmony, unity, and love. It should also produce children, since that is why it was instituted.

The two of you should try to live a Christian life, promoting love between yourselves and toward others. Approach the parish and speak with the priest in charge there; he will help you. *(Letter to Moisés, March 17, 1978)*

To Seek Advice and Dialogue

Sadly, most marriages aren't lived fully in daily life. Infidelity, misunderstanding, problems, etc., destroy them easily because they don't have true Christian roots.

I think you have been separated from your husband for too short a time to begin thinking about getting together with another man, no matter how honest your intentions may be. You could make another mistake. Often, one can only fall into ruin by not seeking counsel in time, or for not wanting to follow it. May the Lord give you light and help you see clearly in your life. Read the gospel; in it you'll find a true source of life. *(Letter to Amalia, March 17, 1978)*

I congratulate you because, as both a mother and wife, you have been able to conduct yourself as a Christian in the face of this critical situation in your home. St. Paul tells us that when a husband fails in faith, the brave example of a virtuous woman is like a light that attracts the rebellious husband to Christian witness.

I suggest that you begin a dialogue with your husband. Try to achieve that when he is in a good mood so as to avoid arguments and be able to speak with him about the Christian peace that existed in your home when you both acted as responsible Christians.

Point out to him that spouses should sanctify each other. The sacrament of marriage imposes this responsibility. Tell him, too, that the children see how you're acting, and that this affects their peace today and in the training they're receiving for the future.

Ask him to analyze your behavior during the years you've been together, so that his jealousy will disappear. On the other hand, you should understand that there are almost always crises in homes, but that they can be overcome. In this case, you are doing what you should. Continue on as a constant example of the Christian woman. *(Letter to Rosa, December 6, 1978)*

Overcome Errors with Patience

Don't despair. Try to be calm. Know that God our Lord understands your strong desire to keep your family intact, and this is sufficient. Pray. Have great faith in the Lord. Keep acting as you have been, with the affection of a wife. Try to overcome your husband's error by living a life which is irreproachable in every sense, not neglecting him or your children.

Your husband will realize that in the street he will never find what he has built at home with you. And sooner or later he will change. Married men often have crises like this one. What is needed here, so that all can return to normal, is the strength of the wife.

Above all, ask Christ to change your husband's behavior and help him understand the damage he is causing. Let prayer be your real consolation. *(Letter to Blanca, December 28, 1978)*

Consecrating Carnal Love

Given the exposure of your family life, I think the most advisable thing for you to do is to legitimize your relationship with your wife. In that way, all of the actions in your home motivated by true Christian love will merit the approval and blessing of God Our Lord.

You will only live in the grace of God united to a woman when that union comes from the sacrament of matrimony.

On the other hand, in order that she not doubt your fidelity, try to avoid any appearance of infidelity, since it is appropriate both to be and to appear faithful. *(Letter to Emilio, November 22, 1978)*

You tell me about your desire to receive communion at Sunday Mass, but you also say that you are living with a woman and have four children whom you love a lot.

Communion is a very important sacrament in the life of a Christian. It includes a commitment that we all live in union. It is a communion with God and with others and the first commitment is with the family.

I advise you to get married in the church, since I see no impediment to doing that, and since you say you love your companion and children. Christian marriage is a seal, with God's blessing, of the love that exists between two Christians. It shows the whole church that in this home there is love, and that love wants to be a likeness of Christ's love for his church, a faithful and productive love, one that implies total self-giving. If you two are in agreement about receiving the blessing of God in your home by marrying in the church, do it soon. *(Letter to Raul M. A., July 14, 1978)*

To Be Generous and Open to Life

It makes me happy that you are not settling for living a married life without its being sanctified by God. It is true that people and human laws see a couple as married when they have had a civil wedding, but what is missing there is the blessing of God, and this you will have if you make your commitment before God's representatives here on earth.

A religious marriage has much greater value, since it has God as witness and as a model of the kind of love you hope to have in your home. That is why a church marriage can't be easily broken. God is the model of fidelity, love, self-giving, mercy, patience, etc. That's how a Christian marriage should be. *(Letter to Miriam F. A., November 4, 1977)*

The environment we live in promotes egotism in people's hearts, which, if accentuated, can lead to really undesirable actions. An example of this is the campaign for sterilization of both women and men.

The church considers sterilization to be a grave offense, since it means denying God the right he has to ask us to collaborate in giving new lives to the world.

The sin you have committed can be forgiven if you repent. Nobody is condemned. What you can do is recommend to others that they not think about being sterilized, but that they go instead to the Office of Population and Family which the church has at their service.

Trust in the mercy of the Lord, which for sinners is limitless. *(Letter to Marta, December 8, 1977)*

Education

Dear children, you are a great hope for our people and our church. Go forward, deepening evermore your Christian commitment.

To live the apostolate of the Eucharist is to be ready to give yourselves to others as Jesus did, to the point of giving your life itself for the good of all. *(Letter to the Children of the Eucharistic Apostolate, May 14, 1979)*

In addition to your studies, try to continue your Christian formation, for only in that way will your studies have true meaning. The church has great hopes for the young. We need young people who are concerned about their fellows and who want to put their knowledge at the service of others. *(Letter to Roque G. C., April 18, 1979)*

Take heart, young man. The great ideals in life are not achieved without a great deal of effort and work. You know that our Lord Jesus, being the Son of God, wanted to share with us this world of work and effort. He goes ahead of us, and invites us to follow him. *(Letter to Nelson R. P., October 2, 1979)*

The Responsibility of Those Who Have Knowledge

In our country there are thousands of people with no opportunity to study, and who live hungering for knowledge, but cannot find anyone concerned about them. Those of us who have studied, if we are Christians, are obliged to "teach those who do not know," and to create favorable conditions in our society so that their need will be satisfied. *(Letter to Fidelina G. R., June 15, 1978)*

Educating children is an arduous and difficult but noble task. It means collaborating with God in forming the human person. That is why mothers and fathers should be concerned not only about the material needs of their children, but above all about their moral, spiritual, and Christian formation. *(Letter to Andres H., July 13, 1979)*

Their formation as Christians is the greatest gift that a mother can give her children, promoting in them feelings of generosity, goodness, and unity. Try to form your children as authentic Christians, Christians generous with others. *(Letter to Margarita del C., March 7, 1979)*

I offer this advice to improve your situation: try to balance your budget better. It seems to me that there is a big difference between the tuition costs for your older daughter (70 colónes) and for the younger (9 colónes). I understand the great sacrifice you're making to have your daughter in an expensive school, but there are other schools which are cheaper but good, and this would solve your problem.

The best way to educate your children is not by putting them in expensive schools, but in being able to prepare them for life: to be generous, kind, just, honorable, and concerned about the others. *(Letter to Carlos H. C., November 4, 1977)*

Death and Resurrection

It was with great sorrow that I received the news first of the sickness and then of the death of your brother. I grew to love him a great deal. Only faith in the Risen Jesus gives us Christians hope of eternal life. This life is fleeting, a short time that the Lord gives us to work on building his reign here. *(Letter to Ines T. S., May 12, 1978)*

Jesus wept at the death of his friend Lazarus, showing his feelings as a human being, at the same time that he resurrected him. We, the followers of Christ, need not be immersed in sorrow, but in the hope that the dead will be raised by the liberating power of Christ. *(Letter to Mercedes H. de F., January 2, 1979)*

I share your deep and appropriate sorrow over the death of your young son in the massacre last May. At that time many homes were, like yours, in mourning.

The Christian hope that sheds a clear light on our pilgrimage through this life consoles us with the great reality that death is our Passover, our passage to finding ourselves definitively with Christ. And in that final encounter and embrace with Christ and the Father, all of our desires and hopes are fully realized. Facing the Father, the enjoyment of this freedom built here on earth is complete, but it will only reach its fullness in the final homeland which is heaven.

I believe that your son in his martyrdom now has this full measure of joy, as I hope you find this objective and Christian thought heartening. The glory of your son can mitigate your pain. In my fraternal prayers, I will always try to comfort you in that pain. *(Letter to Amanda M. C., September 10, 1979)*

You should see death as a natural phenomenon, something that will happen to all of us. We should await it not with anguish but with the certainty and the hope that despite physical death, we will continue to live the true life that the Lord has promised us if we have known how to live his will.

I understand your fear of being alone when you are a person who shares her life with others. I would advise you to stay close to people in need, becoming friends with those who surround you. If you do that, being alone need not be a problem. Read the gospel and reflect on it with others. That will help you take heart in your daily life. I recommend that you read St. Matthew 25. *(Letter to Maria Julia V., November 13, 1978)*

Christians have the great hope that life doesn't end with the death of the body, but that this is a necessary step toward the great freedom we will have in God. What's important is that when we are alive in our bodies, we live as if each day were the last day of our existence. We don't know the time when physical death will arrive, and we must be prepared. *(Letter to Fidelina T. de A., November 4, 1977)*

For us Christians, death is a step toward the Lord in his fullness. Our faith tells us this: we have hope of being resurrected. We have a sure hope in the resurrection because Christ took the first step and will take us with him, those of us who are his disciples—that is, if we have been faithful to the mission he entrusted to us. *(Letter to Francisco Ch. de C., November 15, 1977)*

Part III

FINAL WORDS

◠◡

Monseñor Romero understood his work as a shepherd to mean preaching the gospel, but the circumstances under which he had to preach the gospel made him see that he might have to offer his life like a shepherd for his flock. "A ministry that begins with a Calvary," he writes.

At one time becoming an archbishop meant receiving honors, privilege, courtesy. But Monseñor Romero began receiving curses, contempt, criticism, abandonment by friends and even brothers and sisters. God's words to Isaiah continue to be true: "My ways are not your ways" (Isaiah 55:8).

Monseñor Romero was no less astonished when, upon becoming archbishop of San Salvador, he realized that the road he had envisaged for himself was not the one God had prepared for him. Indeed, Monseñor Romero learned

*to be an archbishop in the pastoral shadow of Monseñor
Luis Chávez y González, who liked to resolve conflicts with
the government by personal visits to the presidents of the
Republic. When Monseñor Romero became archbishop,
this was an easy method for him, because then-President of
the Republic Colonel Arturo Armando Molina was a good
friend of his. But suddenly, a few days after taking up his
post in San Salvador, because of the murder of Father Rutilio
Grande, Monseñor Romero cut off that communication,
regarding it as hypocritical. From then on his watchword
was the same as Christ gave the apostles: "What you hear
whispered, proclaim from the housetops" (Matthew 10:27).*

*Monseñor Romero had to become filled with faith
in order to glimpse that God's ways for him were different from the ones he had imagined for himself. So,
as the faith of Moses is described in Hebrews, we read
from Monseñor Romero's pen, "Every pastor must look
toward the beyond."*

*As a pastor, Monseñor Romero knew how to wait,
convinced that the night will pass and day will come, and
every night of suffering is pregnant with a dawn of resurrection. So he wrote to a friend of his: "I am beginning
to glimpse a new life."*

From the Last Sunday Homily

*On March 23, 1980, the fifth Sunday of Lent, Oscar
Romero preached his last Sunday homily in the Cathedral
of San Salvador.*

Easter is a shout of victory! No one can extinguish that life that Christ resurrected. Not even death and hatred against Him and against His Church will be able to overcome it. He is the victor! Just as He will flourish in an Easter of unending resurrection, so it is necessary also to accompany Him in Lent, in a Holy Week that is cross, sacrifice, martyrdom. . . . Happy are those who do not become offended by His Cross!

Lent, then, is a call to celebrate our redemption in that difficult complex of cross and victory. Our people are very qualified . . . to preach to us of the cross; but all who have Christian faith and hope know that behind this Calvary of El Salvador is our Easter, our resurrection, and that is the hope of the Christian people. . . .

Today, as diverse historical projects emerge for our people, we can be sure that victory will be had by the one that best reflects the plan of God. And this is the mission of the Church . . . to see how the plan of God is being reflected or disdained in our midst. . . .

That is why I ask the Lord during the week, as I gather the cry of the people, the aches of so much crime, and the ignominy of so much violence . . . to call for repentance; and even though I may continue to be a voice crying in the desert, I know that the Church is making the effort to fulfill its mission. . . .

How easy it is to denounce structural injustice, institutionalized violence, social sin! And it is true, this sin is everywhere, but where are the roots of this social sin? In the heart of every human being. Present-day society is a sort of anonymous world in which no one is willing to admit guilt, and everyone is responsible. We are all sinners, and we have all contributed to this massive crime and violence in our country.

Salvation begins with the human person, with human dignity, with saving every person from sin. And in Lent this is God's call: Be converted! . . .

Today El Salvador is living its own Exodus. Today we, too, are journeying to our liberation through the desert, where cadavers and anguished pain are devastating us, and where many suffer the temptation of those who were walking with Moses and wanted to turn back. . . . God desires to save the people making a new history. . . . What is not repeated are the circumstances, the opportunities to which we are witnesses in El Salvador.

History will not perish; God sustains it. That is why I say that in the measure that the historical projects attempt to reflect the eternal project that is God, in that measure they are reflecting the Reign of God, and this is the work of the Church. Because of this, the Church, the people of God in history, is not installed in any one social system, in any political organization, in any political party. . . . She is the eternal pilgrim of history and is indicating at every historical moment what reflects the Reign of God and what does not. She is the servant of the Reign of God. . .

The true solution has to fit into the definitive plan of God. Every solution we seek—a better land distribution, a better administration and distribution of wealth in El Salvador, a political organization structured around the common good of Salvadorans—these must be sought always within the context of definitive liberation. . . . Without God, there can be no true concept of liberation. Temporary liberations, yes; but definitive, solid liberations—only people of faith can reach them. . . .

Do you see how life recovers all of its meaning? And suffering then becomes a communion with Christ, the Christ that suffers, and death is a communion with the death that redeemed the world? Who can feel worthless before this treasure that one finds in Christ, that gives meaning to sickness, to pain, to oppression, to torture, to marginalization? No one is conquered, no one; even though they put you under the boot of oppression and of repression, whoever believes in Christ knows that she is a victor and that the definitive victory will be that of truth and justice! . . .

I would like to appeal in a special way to the men of the Army, and in particular to the troops of the National Guard, the police, and the garrisons. Brothers, you belong to our own people. You kill your own brother peasants; and in the face of an order to kill that is given by a man, the law of God should prevail that says, "Do not kill!" No soldier is obliged to obey an order counter to the law of God. No one has to comply with an immoral law. It is time now that you recover your conscience and obey its dictates rather than the command of sin.

The Church, the defender of the rights of God, of the law of God, of the dignity of the human person, cannot remain silent before so much abomination. We want the government seriously to consider that reforms mean nothing when they come bathed in so much blood. Therefore, in the name of God, and in the name of this long-suffering people, whose laments rise to heaven every day more tumultuous, I beseech you, I beg you, I command you in the name of God: "Stop the repression."

—Translated by Nena Terrell and Sally Hanlon

From the Last Homily of Archbishop Romero

On March 24, 1980, Archbishop Romero celebrated Mass for the first anniversary of the death of Sara Meardi de Pinto, the mother of Jorge Pinto, publisher and editor of El Independiente, a weekly newspaper that was one of the few voices for justice and human rights in El Salvador. The Mass began about 6 p.m. in the chapel of the Divine Providence cancer hospital in El Salvador, where Romero lived. The gospel reading was John 12:23–26:

> *"The hour has come for the Son of Man to be glorified. . . . Unless the grain of wheat falls to*

*the earth and dies, it remains only a grain. But if
it dies, it bears much fruit. Those who love their
own life will lose it; those who hate their own life
in this world will keep it for life eternal. Whoever
wants to serve me must follow me, so that my
servant may be with me where I am."*

Because of the manifold relationship I have had with
the editor of the newspaper *El Independiente,* I am able
to share to some extent his feelings on the anniversary of
his mother's death. Above all, I can appreciate her noble
spirit, how she put all of her educated upbringing, all her
graciousness, at the service of a cause that is so important
now: our people's true liberation.

My dear brothers and sisters, I think we should not
only pray this evening for the eternal rest of our dear
Doña Sarita, but above all we should take to ourselves
her message, one that every Christian ought to want
to live intensely. Many do not understand; they think
Christianity should not be involved in such things. But,
to the contrary, you have just heard in Christ's gospel
that one must not love oneself so much as to avoid getting involved in the risks of life that history demands
of us, and that those who try to fend off the danger will
lose their lives, while those who out of love for Christ
give themselves to the service of others will live, like the
grain of wheat that dies, but only apparently. If it did
not die, it would remain alone. The harvest comes about

only because it dies, allowing itself to be sacrificed in the earth and destroyed. Only by undoing itself does it produce the harvest. . . .

This is the hope that inspires us Christians. We know that every effort to better society, especially when injustice and sin are so ingrained, is an effort that God blesses, that God wants, that God demands of us. Doña Sarita was that kind of generous person, and her attitude was embodied in her son Jorge and in all those who work for these ideas. Of course, we must try to purify these ideals, Christianize them, clothe them with the hope of that which lies beyond. That makes them stronger because it gives us the assurance that all that we cultivate on earth, if we nourish it with Christian hope, will never be a failure. We will find it in a purer form in that kingdom where our merit will be in the labor we have done here on earth. . . .

Dear brothers and sisters, let us all view these matters at this historic moment with that hope, that spirit of giving and of sacrifice. Let us all do what we can. We can all do something, at least have a sense of understanding and sympathy. The holy woman we remember today could not do many things directly perhaps, but she did encourage those who can work, sympathized with their struggle, and above all prayed. Even after her death, she sends a message from eternity that it is worthwhile to labor, because all those longings for justice, peace, and well-being that we experience on earth become realized for us if we enlighten them with Christian hope. We know that no one can go on forever, but those who have put into their work a sense of very great faith, of love of God, of hope among human beings, find it all results in the splendors of a crown that is the sure reward of those who labor thus, cultivating truth, justice, love, and gooiness on the earth. Such labor does not remain here below, but purified by God's Spirit, is harvested for our reward.

This holy Mass now, this Eucharist, is just such an act of faith. To Christian faith at this moment the voice of diatribe appears changed for the body of the Lord, who offered himself for the redemption of the world, and in this chalice the wine is transformed into the blood that was the price of salvation. May this body immolated and this blood sacrificed for humans nourish us also, so that we may give our body and our blood to suffering and to pain—like Christ, not for self, but to bring about justice and peace for our people.

Let us join together, then, intimately in faith and hope at this moment of prayer for Doña Sarita and ourselves.

At this moment, a shot rang out in the chapel and Archbishop Romero fell mortally wounded. He died within minutes.

—Translated by Michael J. Walsh

AFTERWORD

The Life and Death of Oscar Romero

Monseñor Ricardo Urioste

For me, it is both easy and hard to speak of Archbishop Romero. It is easy in the sense that I knew him, dealt with him, and could see the profundity of his life, the spirit of union with God that was the root of his entire existence—not just in his years as archbishop, but in his first years as a student, in his early priesthood, and in all the rest of his ministry.

Msgr. Ricardo Urioste, who died on January 15, 2016, was named vicar general of the Archdiocese of San Salvador by Archbishop Oscar Romero; he was one of Romero's closest collaborators. This article, based on a talk given at the Jesuit University (UCA) in San Salvador to mark the tenth anniversary of Romero's death, was originally published in the March 23, 1990, issue of *Commonweal*.

But it is hard because his death still overwhelms me. He was a great man, a great priest, a great bishop, murdered because of the ignominy and injustice of this country.

Archbishop Romero's homilies have already been published, and this year, at the tenth anniversary of his death, we will also be publishing his journal, which he tape recorded each night. But there's also something else which, I believe, is a great treasure: the notes he made during his retreats, where he opened his soul before God, before himself, and before the events of the times.

In one of his retreat notebooks there is the phrase, "I will dine with him." This comes from the Apocalypse (3:20). In the New Testament the Apocalypse is the book of the martyrs. And it is about the martyrdom of Archbishop Romero that I wish to speak. I think the Apocalypse is the only book in the entire New Testament that speaks of the martyrs and of martyrdom. Of course, the gospels speak of Jesus as the one who gives his life, who hands over his life, and he is, you might say, the prototype of the martyr. As we know, two kinds of accusations against Jesus appear in the gospels. One kind is religious: that he claimed he was God. The other is political: that he was subverting the people. The accusation of being "political" is as old as Christianity, as ancient as Christ. There's nothing strange or surprising about it, and it was one of the accusations that was also made all the time against Archbishop Romero.

In the Letter to the Hebrews we learn that without the shedding of blood there is no redemption, there is no salvation. John, in the Apocalypse, is distilling all the thought of the church of that time about martyrdom. He is writing at a time when the church was being persecuted in some places, and the aim of the Apocalypse is to buoy up persecuted Christians. It describes Jesus as the faithful witness, that is, as the martyr.

The martyr is the faithful witness. Our word "witness" comes from a Greek word which means "martyr." Where we see "be my witnesses in all places," in Greek it says "be my martyrs." Later the word "martyr" began to be applied to those who, because they were witnesses, gave their blood for Christ and the faith. I would say that death is not a biological event but a theological event: the death of a Christian is a theological event, and that is how we should see it. That is how Archbishop Romero saw it, and that is how it's seen by those who are faithful witnesses to the truth.

In the Apocalypse (6:9ff.) John says, "When he opened the fifth seal, I saw under the altar the souls of those who had been slain for the word of God and for the witness they had borne; they cried out with a loud voice, 'O Sovereign Lord, holy and true, how long before thou wilt judge and avenge our blood on those who dwell upon the earth?'" This is the definition of "martyr" John gives. The Roman Empire didn't care if the early Christians were defending the divinity of Christ or the Trinity; it cared about the fact that they didn't adore the idols, that they were subverting the empire.

John also says the martyrs protest to God: "Lord, when will you do justice. . . ?" (6:10). We might direct ourselves to God at this moment as well. After such torrents of blood have been shed, after seventy thousand people have been murdered, including seventeen priests, four nuns, and an archbishop, where is justice? In this country, this democratic, Christian country, we carry on as if nothing had happened. Other countries, right here in Central America, that are not democratic or Christian haven't killed a single priest or nun.

In response to those who ask, when will there be justice, John sees that the persecution is going to continue, that people will continue to die, but that it's necessary to continue witnessing to the faith, because for the Christian death should be a vocation. Just as death is a theological and not a biological event, so too for the Christian who gives and wants to give himself in true witness, death is a vocation, a call. The last reference I'll make to the Apocalypse (from chapter 3) is to the phrase we found in Archbishop Romero's retreat notes: "And I will dine with him." Verses 19-20 say: "Take heart and be converted. I am at the door and calling; if someone listens to my voice and opens the door, I will enter and dine with him. I with him and he with me."

Yet we should be very clear on one thing: we are not to seek martyrdom. What we should aim for is a life of witness. We should seek a life which really gives the kind of witness that's needed, but we should not seek martrydom itself.

We should also be very clear on what the criteria are for determining who is a genuine martyr. The first is that God is present as the root and summit of the person's life. Second, the person has been connected with other people. That is, we're not just talking about a vertical relationship with God, about a person who's spent his or her whole life singing alleluias, and has known God only in that way. We're talking about someone who has also discovered God in other people. This is absolutely necessary. Third, the giving over of one's entire life to the Christian ideal—that your whole life revolves around the ideal that Christ offers us. And the fourth, I would say, is the acceptance of death for the faith itself.

These four elements were present in the life of Archbishop Romero. It's been said that the degree to which a tree flowers depends on how deeply it's rooted in the ground. That was Archbishop Romero—someone who flowered because he was so deeply rooted in God. For him God was the absolute. He made God the infinite in his life. He tried to communicate all this to others, to share it with them. What most impressed one about Archbishop Romero was his capacity for encounter with God, his ability to root his life totally in God. That was the source of his strength and his vitality. A journalist once asked him, "Where do you get the strength to carry on in spite of everything?" Archbishop Romero answered, "You ask at an opportune moment, because I've just returned from my retreat. That's where I find the energy and the strength."

I saw this myself on many occasions. I remember one time, in December 1979 at the *Hospitalito* [the Divine Providence Hospital, where Archbishop Romero lived, and was later killed]. It was early in the morning, at breakfast time, and the archbishop was being visited by Cardinal Lorscheider of Brazil and a member of the civilian-military junta which, at that moment, was governing El Salvador. At one point, Archbishop Romero got up and left. Now, I knew those men had come there to see him, not me, so eventually I got up and went looking for him. I went to his apartment, but he wasn't there; I went to the visitors' room, the kitchen and the garden, but he wasn't there either. Finally, it occurred to me to look in the chapel, and there he was, kneeling before the Blessed Sacrament, which was exposed. I went up to him and said, "They're waiting for you." And he said, "That's okay. They can wait. I'll be coming."

I think that Archbishop Romero never said anything, never did anything, without first consulting with God. That's why he was sure of what he said. He didn't care what the accusations and the threats were, he was sure of the things he'd said because he had been in dialogue with God about them. This was a man who had discovered that the root of his existence, of his whole being—as a person, as a priest, as a bishop—was God.

I remember another time when we went to Rome together. As soon as we got there, after traveling all night long, he invited me to go to the Basilica of St. Peter. The confessional altar, where the tomb of Peter is said to be, is right at the entrance to the basilica. He knelt down right there and began to pray. I knelt too, but after ten minutes I got up. But he continued for another twenty minutes, totally absorbed in prayer.

When I'm asked what it was about Archbishop Romero that I most admire, I've always answered: the sanctity of his priestly life, his unity with God, his interior life and spirit, because everything else that he was came from all that. For me, that's the kind of person who is really convincing; someone like that can really bring people along, not just by words but by the person's life itself, which gives this witness.

Archbishop Romero was very faithful to his spiritual life. He went to confession every week, and he consulted with his spiritual director. He sought out guidance for what he was doing. Like all holy men and women who have felt the mystery of sin, he felt the mystery of our freedom, which is capable of saying "yes" but also of saying "no." He had the humility to seek God with patience. All this is something which appears very rarely, and that is what made Archbishop Romero capable of being a prophet.

Now, prophets aren't innovators, and Archbishop Romero was no innovator. The prophets are those who speak of the eternal things, as they apply at the moment.

The prophet always speaks of God and of the circumstances in which we find ourselves. The prophet speaks of respect for life, and that is older than the first page of the Bible. The prophet, then, in a certain sense is the great conservative, the one who wants to conserve the great values that God has given us.

Archbishop Romero spoke like this, and when he did he was accused of getting involved in politics. There's nothing that makes me think more of how unjust and stupid people can be. He spoke out about all the people who had been tortured, massacred, and hurled into rivers. That isn't getting involved in politics; that is speaking of the Fifth Commandment: Thou shalt not kill. Every prophet, every bishop, every priest is obliged to speak out like that. The prophet is the one who is faithful to God, who says, God is asking this of me, and I'm going to do it, while others say, "Who knows, this could be dangerous, and you know, you've got to be prudent."

We speak a lot about the virtue of prudence, but not so much about the virtues of fortitude and justice. The prophet is imprudent because God was imprudent, because Jesus was imprudent. Because if our Lord hadn't said what he said, they wouldn't have crucified him, either. As a prophet, Archbishop Romero was able to cleanse the language. He revived the truth, made it heard, and many believe that is why he was killed. The truth, in countries like ours, will always have such consequences. There were those who couldn't tolerate the truth Archbishop Romero proclaimed, just as there were those who couldn't tolerate the truth that Jesus proclaimed.

It is the absolutizing of God which enables us to see other people and their situations clearly. St. Mark tells the story of the blind man cured by Jesus who, when asked if he could see, replied, "I see people, but they look like trees." He couldn't see them well. When we're not capable of seeing people in their true situations, we're seeing them as trees. The people are suffering, going hungry, being repressed, enduring so many other things, but for us they can be like trees, like things. But the prophet is one who sees people and their situations as they really are, who feels intimately the things that are going on around him and isn't able to just let them continue. He is the one who suffers those things, just as Jeremiah and Isaiah and all the true prophets suffered.

The prophet is one whose very existence is a sign, and who lives the values of the Kingdom in his or her personal and community life. He or she is also one who carries on in faith, in spite of all misunderstandings. It was like that with Archbishop Romero. Many of us—for fear or whatever other reason—criticized him, judged him, abandoned him. It reached the point where one day he said, "Even if I wind up all alone, I'm going to carry on." And even today we're still afraid to have a picture of him or a book about him in our houses.

I don't want to conclude without mentioning some things he wrote during his last retreat. He died on March

24, 1980, and February 25 of that year he began his last
retreat. And this [Msgr. Urioste holds up a simple school-
child's notebook]—I even tremble when I touch it—is
where he wrote his notes during that retreat. He wrote
about his death—let us say, he wrote about his martyrdom.

In one place, for example, he says, "I feel afraid of
violence. I've been warned about serious threats against
me for this coming week." That is to say, he felt fear, just as
Jesus did in Gethsemani. The scripture writers tell us that
this, even more than the crucifixion, was the most difficult
part of Jesus' Passion, when he saw there in Gethsemani
all that was going to happen to him.

Archbishop Romero was convinced that he was going
to be killed. And nevertheless he writes, honestly and
humbly, "I feel afraid of violence. I fear the weakness
of my flesh, but I ask the Lord to give me serenity and
perseverance." In other words, he's in no way disposed to
take even one step backward, even though he knows that
if he carries on, he's going to be killed. He was offered
the chance to leave the country, he was offered all kinds
of positions in various places, but he said, no, I'm going
to stay here.

In another place he writes, "Father Azcue came and
heard my confession." Father Azcue was his last spiritual director, and on the day he was killed, Archbishop
Romero went to have Father Azcue hear his confession.
Later, Father Azcue said Archbishop Romero had told him
that day, "I want to feel clean before God." The faithful

witness wants to feel clean before God and, of course, before the people. And on this same page in his retreat notebook, he criticizes himself for "not being careful enough about my confessions and my spiritual life," and then he remakes his life plan, and among the specific things he mentions are, "Get up at midnight to pray." He also mentions "disciplines," by which he means punishing himself physically (I think this must mean mortification of the flesh), things like fasting on Fridays, things that you and I don't do but which were vital for him. They helped make him who he was.

On this same page in his retreat notebook, he writes, "My other fear is about the risks for my life." He feared, he knew, he foresaw his death. He was receiving all kinds of threats at that time, even public ones. The ads in the newspapers against him in those days were, in effect, threats. But there were others that were even more clear. And there was another sign that he was certain he was going to be killed.

When a bishop dies a group of priests is in charge of naming an interim successor to serve until the new bishop is named. Now, Archbishop Romero had said he wanted three more priests added to this group. And I remember one day at the *Hospitalito*—we were having a meeting there, and it was about ten or twelve days before he was killed—and he asked us, "Have you done the paperwork to have the three priests added?" We had not. He stood up and said, "Do it, and do it now!" Later on, after his death, we remembered that incident, and we said to ourselves, "Well, he knew. . . ."

On another page in his notebook, he wrote, "It's hard for me to accept the violent death which, in these circumstances, seems very possible. The papal nuncio of Costa Rica has warned me about imminent dangers for this coming week. My disposition"—and here remember the criteria we mentioned earlier for a genuine martyrdom, especially the accepting of the Christian ideal and the willingness to give one's life for the faith itself—"should be to give my life for God, however it should end. The grace of God will enable us to live through the unknown circumstances. He aided the martyrs and, if it should be necessary that I die as they did, I will feel him very close to me at the moment of breathing my last breath. But more important than the moment of death is to give him all my life and live for him and for my own mission." He is not seeking out martyrdom. He sought to live a life of witness.

Later he writes, "In this way I make concrete my consecration to the heart of Jesus, which has always been the source of inspiration and Christian joy in my life. And I put all my life under his loving Providence, and with faith in him I accept my death, however difficult it may be."

He doesn't offer his life for something in particular. "I don't want to state an intention, for example for peace in my country or for the flowering of our church." Why does he take this position? Because he has his roots deeply in God, even at the moment of his death. "Because," he says, "the heart of Christ will know how to give my life the meaning it requires."

He ends with these words: "To be happy, for me it is enough to know for sure that he is in my life and in my death. And in spite of my sins, I have put my trust in him and I will not be confounded," he quotes a psalm. "And others will carry on the work of the church and the country with more wisdom and more sanctity."

So he dined with the Lord, and now he's with him and with our church and with our country. He's also with the poor, whom he defended so much and for whom he died. I always say that Archbishop Romero was martyred for his love for the poor, for defending them, and for the magisterium of the church. That magisterium is very clear: it says the church should make a preferential option for the poor. To really love the poor requires concrete actions.

—Translated by Gene Palumbo